LOVE

A Psychotherapist Explains How to

Cure Yourself of Depression

Michael Sclater

For feedback, comments and suggestions for later editions please email Michael@sclater.co.uk

LOVE

Caring about and enjoying relating with everyone and everything.

And loving everything you do.

Praise for the Book

"Michael Sclater's book is simultaneously very practical and very deep. The author draws on his many years as a psychotherapist as well as his expertise on contemplative traditions to draw together explanations and advice on addressing depression. For me, however, it wasn't just a book about depression itself, it was also a book about living well. The insights into the mind, both its conscious and unconscious workings, were helpful in identifying some of the challenges of living in our current era and the ways we often don't help ourselves seek the very things which are most likely to engage us with life.

Sclater's response is kind and also at times, quite direct, in guiding us to wisdom which, through the ages, has helped people live with more wisdom and love. The book is also a challenge to a mental health system, often so busy and overstretched, that people are not encouraged to look at the causes of their feelings and their suffering.

Sclater encourages us to stop feeling scared of feelings, but to notice them, to be curious, using this curiosity as a way back to living in a more integrated and engaged way. I would highly recommend this book. It's rare to find a fresh voice on a complex subject; this is a book that could make a difference."

Rhian Taylor

Contents

Introduction

This book describes practical things that you can do to cure yourself of depression. You can do them on your own or, better still, with the support of friends or professionals.

The way out of depression described here comes from more than 20 years' experience of treating people for depression. My observation is that the people who manage to do the kinds of things described here get better and go on to enjoy their lives. Those who don't, unfortunately, rarely do.

I hope that you will find this book especially helpful if you have tried currently available treatments but found they didn't really help. This way out of depression is different. Instead of trying to fix whatever is supposedly wrong in your *brain* - by means of drugs or some form of therapy - it focuses much more on whatever might be wrong in your *life* that is making you depressed. When you can fix the problem in your life your brain will be fine and you will be happy.

Problems in life can take many forms, but they all ultimately come down to one really big problem. This is a life without enough love. That includes love for one's self, love for others and even love for the whole adventure of life itself.

Love is the driving force common to all humanity. It's the only thing that can make life worth living and also hugely enjoyable. When we love, we want to spend time with others and to have lots of wonderful relationships. When we love what we are doing we find we have limitless energy. When we love, we get fully involved in life and then meaning and motivation arise spontaneously. When we love ourselves, others, activities, other creatures and the planet itself that's when we can say we are having a lovely time.

Depression happens when we get so knocked about by life that love collapses. That's when we withdraw from social contact, lose our energy, meaning and motivation – and feel terrible. So the central theme of all the things you can do to get out of depression is to rediscover love. That's what this book will enable you to do.

We will pay special attention to five main aspects of love: love for yourself, love for others, willingness to be loved, love for what you do all day and love for the whole incredibly challenging business of life itself.

Of course you already know many of the things described in this book. In those cases you can just check that you actually do them. With the things that are new, you will find that you do not need to completely achieve them in order to feel better; you will be happier the moment you begin to take positive steps in the right direction.

By the way, nothing in this book is original to me. People around the world have known it all for millennia. If you are lucky enough to have a wise and radiant old grandmother you can be sure she knows it all too. I am just writing down ancient wisdom that recent fashions in treatment have caused so many to lose sight of.

Please enjoy messing this book up with notes, comments, drawings, plans of action etc. It's a workbook not just a book to study. The great thing is to try to actually do things. Just talking about depression isn't likely to help.

PART 1

How to Begin – Even If You've Just About Lost Hope

Key points

Decide to love

Switch on your energy

A good way to think about getting out of depression is as a highly enjoyable adventure of doing new things, learning new skills, bringing wonderful new things into your life and finding out what really brings you joy. It isn't even particularly difficult.

The difficult bit is to bring yourself to actually set out on the adventure. That's because of two unfortunate common symptoms of depression which are hopelessness (or at the very least absence of optimism) and possibly very genuine feelings of exhaustion. In order to get over these obstacles here are two incredibly important things for you to do:

Decide to love

It is very possible that, due to things having gone badly in your life either recently or long ago, your unconscious mind has to some extent given up on its deepest desire and longing, which is to love and be loved. That would be why you might not feel like seeing friends, looking after your health, being creative, contributing to your community, doing anything much or getting fully involved in life.

What you need to do now is take a life changing and momentous decision. This is to decide to love. That's it. You need to do this even if some awful experience has left you in a state of despair or a cold fury about life and everything.

From now on you are going to do your best to love other people, yourself (unconditionally – faults and all), animals, plants, the planet, the climate, snakes, crocodiles and even the whole incredibly challenging and sometimes painful business of life itself. You are even going to love people you dislike or fervently disagree with. In fact, everything. Of course getting good at this is a lifetime's project, but you can decide now to make a start. Nothing could be more fun. It will make life worthwhile. So, can you decide to begin to love more and more as each day passes? Can you decide this even though you may have been through some bad (and possibly extremely loveless) times?

As soon as you begin to reawaken your love, you can expect the following to begin to happen:

- You see the beauty in people. You won't be so influenced by their possible faults and shortcomings.
- You appreciate the beauty in yourself.

- Love comes to you.
- While keeping your wits about you, you discover that you can trust.
- Lots of warm relationships.
- Joy (arises when you love any activity).

By the way, our need to love is not necessarily anything to do with religion. Religions (at their best) simply point us in the direction of an inescapable psychological need.

You can take the first steps to more love with the aid of your brain. That is to say, you will use rational thinking to decide to do it. Then you use your will to actually do it. You will see later in the book that further - even bigger - steps happen in your heart. That's a fascinating and ancient science which can bring even more joy into your life.

Switch on your energy

A characteristic of being depressed is that you may very genuinely feel that you don't have any energy. Maybe you can hardly get off the sofa or change the television channel. The idea of beginning to take all kinds of positive action to get out of depression can seem totally unrealistic.

Well, it could be that you really do have something physically seriously wrong with you; you can ask your doctor to check this out. However, the fact is that you almost certainly do have energy, but it has got blocked. It is there somewhere in the core of your being but just isn't welling up into all kinds of joyful activity and enthusiasm.

If you doubt this, you could try a simple thought experiment. Imagine you are lying exhausted on the sofa and all of a sudden see flames racing towards you. You will be out of the house as fast as a greyhound out of the starting blocks. So you do have energy. It was just stuck.

You can forcibly kickstart your energy into flowing again by means of vigorous exercise. To do this you will need to override any signals that are coming from your brain to the effect that you are too tired and miserable to do anything. The faculty that you can use to do this is Will. You know what will is. It is what you use when the alarm goes off on a miserable February morning and every neuron in your brain says 'Stay in bed' - but a higher part of your consciousness says 'You need to go to work'.

The type of exercise you choose needs to really fire you up. If you can possibly afford a personal trainer, or some kind of supportive group, to help you get going this will make it a whole lot easier and more fun.

To begin with you may find getting moving a real struggle. Just work through this. In a short time you will feel more alive and soon you will find yourself feeling miserable any time you don't exercise.

If you doubt the importance of exercise, here is a summary of what current research tells us about its benefits:

- Exercise reduces depression and anxiety.
- Exercise boosts the levels of chemicals in the brain that make us feel good such as serotonin, dopamine, noradrenaline and endorphins.
- Exercise reduces the levels of stress hormones such as adrenaline and cortisol.
- Exercise has been found to stimulate the growth of neurons in certain brain regions damaged by depression.
- Increased self-esteem.
- Improved sleep.
- A sense of achievement.
- Less anger or frustration.
- A healthy appetite.
- Reduced sensitivity to pain e.g. back pain.
- Better social life.

L O V E

Here is a quote from a psychiatrist at Harvard University:

'Exercise is the single best thing you can do for your brain in terms of mood, memory and learning.'

Exercises to choose from

The gym is the obvious option for most. Available everywhere and not too expensive.

Cycling.

Dance such as salsa, tango, Zumba, belly dancing, flamenco, breakdancing, line dancing.

Ball games like football, badminton, tennis, squash so long as you are good enough to really fire up your system.

Exercise routines such as Pilates, dynamic yoga, aerobics, Nia, Five Rhythms.

Running, vigorous walking.

Morning exercise in the park such as Tai Chi, Chi Gung, Yoga.

Adventure sports.

Climbing, kayaking, skydiving.

Rowing, canoeing, surfing.

Singing with others. Singing might not seem like vigorous exercise but it has a similar energy - rousing effect. It does involve effort and breathing.

Boxing and martial arts. These can have a special advantage because they develop an ability to stand up for yourself and get what you want.

ACTION

Decide to love.

Fire up your energy.

PART 2

Love Your Health

Key points

Exercise

Eat well

Sleep well

Breathe well

Money

I realise that you may be impatient to find out just exactly what you can do right now to stop being depressed. Well, you might find it rather boring, but the first thing to do is to make sure that you have in place the fundamentals for any kind of health (mental or physical).

As a psychotherapist I have reached the point where I don't really see much point in seeing anyone who isn't willing to put in place the basic foundations for mental and physical health. Without them, you could see the most brilliant therapist in the world, win a superyacht or live in paradise itself and still be miserable. That's how important they are.

Even if you are in a hurry to fix whatever is making you unhappy, please make sure that you are paying attention to these 5 essential things:

Continue with exercise

We humans suffer from what one might call 'Ferrari Syndrome'. We are high performance machines. You exist because your ancestors were so superbly good at hunting animals, finding food, farming, working and even fighting when necessary that they managed to produce and rear children and eventually you. Just like a supercar, if you run all the time on a slow ahead setting you will cease to function properly. Your body is designed to run fast and achieve amazing things.

So, no matter where you live or what your lifestyle is, you need regular exercise if you are to be fully well, active and happy.

Hints

If you are currently unfit, overweight and maybe hopelessly unathletic you might feel embarrassed when you turn up for exercise. In fact, people will admire you!

You might feel worse, not better, to begin with. But this soon turns around. In a few weeks you will find yourself feeling miserable any time you don't exercise.

Eat well

Just as a car needs to run on the fuel it is designed for, so we human beings need the right kind of food to function healthily and efficiently. When you eat well, you feel better, so it's true to say that:

Good food = good mood.

Bad food = bad mood.

Eat food that is fresh and freshly prepared whenever you can. If you eat food that is old, stale, lifeless and contaminated, you yourself will feel old, stale, lifeless and contaminated.

It takes a bit of willpower to resist the pressures on us to eat junk food, readymade food and takeaways and to drink just about any liquid chemical fluid other than water. Just remember that these foods often contain enormous quantities of fat, salt and sugar with the possible addition of antibiotic and pesticide residues, colourings, preservatives and other various chemicals.

If you are already a skilled cook you will know how to feed yourself properly. In case you aren't, here is a simple way to feed yourself well:

Breakfast - instead of processed breakfast cereals or toast you could try porridge or muesli. Alternatively, boil up some rice – enough to keep for a few days in the fridge. Each morning make up a bowl with rice, any fruit, nuts, raisins and yoghurt. It's delicious, cheap and will keep you going all morning. Coffee and tea can be useful stimulants but remember to drink plenty of water (comes free out of the tap) during the day.

Lunch - any meat, fish, rice or potatoes left over from last night's supper. Make a salad (lettuce and any other green stuff). If you're out at work you can take a box with you. If you're eating out, just order something healthy.

Snacks - fruit and nuts.

Dinner - a small (e.g. half) portion of fish or meat. You don't need huge quantities of protein and eating less helps the environment too. Then lots of vegetables, plus potato or rice. If you're vegetarian, then even more vegetables. Cheese if you like. A lot of people seem to feel better if they buy gluten-free bread and even avoid wheat altogether.

If you are a cook the above may seem embarrassingly simple and boring. But if you aren't, it is a way to feel good on a daily basis with an absolute minimum of time, effort and cost.

If you eat well and exercise, you are most unlikely to have to worry about your weight. You may even lose weight because a lot of 'fat' is actually junk that the body is storing because it can't use it.

Hints

When you start to eat well, your energy may dip initially or even for a week or two. This is because your body is getting used to the change. But you will soon feel (and probably look) like a different person.

You can expect to enjoy good food more and more as you get used to it. Eventually, junk tastes disgusting.

Always check the ingredients of anything you buy. Read the labels especially carefully if you see words like 'Health' or 'Eco'. They may mean just the opposite. Food manufacturers do not exist in order to benefit your health; they exist to make money for their shareholders.

Sleep well

Too little sleep, or irregular sleep, can be a straightforward cause of depression. If you don't get enough, no amount of medication or therapy will cure your depression.

If you do shift work, work irregular hours or work frequently at night these may be the sole cause of your depression. It can happen that a person undergoes all kinds of treatment for depression, such as antidepressants or some form of therapy, when all they needed was to achieve regular sleep at night. Could this be happening to you?

One thing you can do is to make sure you have a holiday of two or preferably three uninterrupted weeks, sleep regularly at night and see what happens. If your mood improves, you are going to have to do everything you possibly can to find a job with regular hours.

Of course there are some jobs which really do have to be done sometimes at night, such as nursing or the police. If that works for you, that's fine. But if it is making you depressed the only solution may be to try to change or at least radically renegotiate your job.

What could stop you?

Too little sleep may be arising from unconscious attitudes in you. Here are some that you could check that you don't have:

- You need the extra money. Are you sure that you couldn't manage with less? Is the extra money worth the price of ruining your health – and possibly relationships too?

- Are you putting up with being exploited? Is your employer making a fortune out of unnecessarily ruining your health? How many jobs really need to be done in the small hours of the night?

- Is it possible you have been persuaded that there is something exciting about a 24/7 society? Might there be better sources of excitement than ruining your health?

- Do you think there is merit in being busy for as many of the 24 hours as possible? If so what exactly is it? Is business the only thing that matters in life?

- Do you think sleep is a waste of time?

Finally, two things may help you get a better night's sleep. First, see what happens if you don't drink alcohol or coffee in the evening and don't eat just before bed. Second, using your body as well as your mind throughout the day may well help you sleep better.

You can see later that, if you learn to meditate, you can learn to switch your mind off on those occasions when it rushes around pointlessly and hyperactively in circles. You can use this ability to shut it up if it keeps you awake at night.

Breathe well

You might think that breathing well comes naturally. It probably did when you were a child. But stress, tension and acquired bad habits can cause breathing to be very limited and constricted. The results of this can be a general reduction of vitality, panic attacks and inability to cope with frightening or challenging situations.

You can change this by following some simple exercises to increase vitality and energy:

- Lie on your back on the floor. Rest a hand gently on your belly (i.e. just below your tummy button).

- As you breathe in, allow the hand on your belly to rise several inches as lots of air flows in.

  By relaxing all the muscles around your chest and belly, you can enable the whole of your lungs to fill. If you haven't done this before, you will discover that your lungs are much larger and reach much further down than you might have realised. You are now taking in more oxygen with every breath. Notice that you don't have to do any work to breathe in - the lungs are elastic and fill by themselves.

- Breathe out, using the muscles in your belly to gently squeeze it in so you feel as if it's going to meet your spine at the back. Feel your hand drop several inches.

  You can exaggerate these movements for a few breaths to help you get the idea. As your belly goes in, it squeezes every last molecule of air and waste products out of your lungs. Practice for a bit.

- Now, as you breathe in, check that your diaphragm (the sheet of muscle below your ribs) drops down (towards your feet) making even more space for your lungs. Don't be hard on yourself if you notice that for the last few years it has got into the habit of doing the opposite.

- As you breathe out, check that your diaphragm moves up into your chest cavity pushing even more waste product out of your lungs. Again, don't worry if you notice that your diaphragm was working just about exactly backwards! It happens easily, especially when we get stressed. See if you can get it going the right way again.

  Practice a bit more.

- Now for some finishing touches. As you breathe in, feel the air first of all flow all the way down as if it's ending up in your belly. Then feel it fill up your lower chest, middle chest and eventually upper chest. Let the air into the back of your chest as well as the front. It's like filling a jug with water - from the bottom up.

- As you breathe out, experience the reverse. The air leaves your upper chest, middle chest, lower chest and eventually your belly.

After a while you may notice that you can breathe more slowly than before; that's because you are now breathing more efficiently. You are likely to feel calmer and stronger.

Although it is easiest to practice breathing like this lying down for the first few times, you can actually practice anywhere - during boring meetings, when driving, watching TV etc.

Breathing well will help lift your depression, but it will have other advantages as well. These include preventing panic attacks, helping with asthma, keeping calm in difficult, dangerous and stressful situations, improving your ability in any sport and feeling generally calmer and stronger.

Money

Ongoing worry about money is enough to make anyone depressed. So, if this is happening to you, an important question is whether there could be any way of reducing this worry. Here are some possibilities that you might find helpful:

Know the exact situation

When the money situation is bad, the prospect of really focusing on it can seem increasingly scary. However, you will feel better if you can somehow force yourself to work out what your exact situation is. You will feel better even if the situation is awful. Find some sheets of paper (or suitable computer software) and do this:

- List your monthly outgoings. You can do this by looking at what you spent last month and the one before.

In your monthly expenditure, include an allocation for any expenses that you pay annually instead of monthly such as insurance, car tax etc.

- Now list your income - all the money you know will come in whether from work or other sources. Deduct the first figure from the second. The difference is your exact situation – either positive, or negative.

- Now, taking your courage in both hands, list any debts – credit cards etc.

  Knowing exactly what the situation is will be much less stressful than not knowing. And it will help you to...

- Take action

  Somehow, you need to close any gap between your outgoings and income. Obviously, earning more would be great. Any chance of overtime or even some extra work somewhere? Have you applied for any help that you are entitled to?

- Next, it's going to be a question of spending less until you've got rid of that gap. If you treat this as a creative project you will find that it can actually be enjoyable. And you will be amazed at how much you can save by the cumulative effect of what might seem to be insignificant steps. You could begin by cutting out things like:
  - Takeaway coffees
  - Ready meals
  - Eating out
  - Drinks in pubs
  - Betting
  - Alcohol, drugs, cigarettes
  - Processed food
  - Bottled water
  - Fizzy drinks
  - TV that you have to pay for
  - Amazon Prime
  - Buying new instead of from charity shops
  - Competing with others who are better off (or seem to be - they may just be heavily in debt)
  - Expensive toys and presents
  - Buying anything because a marketing person wants you to buy it
  - Any standing orders you have forgotten about
  - A car that does more then get you from one place to another.

Remember to make time to obtain competitive quotes for every single service (e.g. gas, electricity, oil, internet, phones, banking, insurance) at least once a year. You could save thousands in this way.

If necessary, obtain professional help to try to renegotiate any debts. You may be surprised at how possible this is. It is not in a creditor's interest for you to default.

If these savings are not enough you are going to have to consider cutting something big (and painful – but less painful than financial crisis) such as:

o Holiday
o Car
o Dwelling size or location

- Check your attitude to money

Some people get into trouble with money because, more or less consciously, they hate it. Or they pay too little attention to it because they consider other things more enjoyable or important. If this could be the case for you, consider what money actually is.

In a tiny minority of people money is a vehicle for greed, gambling, manipulation, power, control, exploitation and worse. But in the ordinary world which most of us inhabit money is a recognition of love. It's what you give to the farmer who produced your food, the shop that sold it, the electricity people who fixed the cables at 2am in a storm, the rubbish collectors, the person who got your computer to work and the engineer who fixed the broken down train. Money is what people give to you for your contribution. Money is a convenient way of recognising what people do for each other.

If you have difficulties around money, take some time to explore what attitudes you have. See if you can trace where they came from. Are they helpful? If not, what might you put in their place?

Here are some examples of common unhelpful attitudes to money that are likely to lead to problems, stress and eventual depression:

- o I hate money – so I try to ignore it
- o My family have always been clueless about money
- o I have to have the same as everyone else

- ○ I'll be happy if I have this (usually works for a few hours)
- ○ It's embarrassing to have anything that isn't new
- ○ I don't want unfashionable old stuff
- ○ I feel more confident wearing /buying a known brand
- ○ Everyone has pay TV/a fast car/holidays abroad etc
- ○ If I don't have enough money I can borrow some
- ○ Gambling might solve my problem
- ○ The universe will look after me
- ○ I don't have time to cook
- ○ I can get it on my credit card
- ○ The kids have to have this
- ○ Someone else owes me a living
- ○ Money is the root of all evil
- ○ I'm not really worth paying much
- ○ I don't like negotiating
- ○ I don't have time to manage my money
- ○ Money is boring
- ○ I don't deserve to be paid properly
- ○ My partner will leave if I don't spend enough on him/her.

LOVE

ACTION

Even if you are currently depressed and not feeling like doing anything, sort out your money.

Decide to enjoy money and managing it.

PART 3

Love Yourself

Key points

Be OK

Love your feelings

Love your anger

Forgive

Aim forwards

Do what you have to do

Check your psychological environment

Check your physical environment

Search for joys

Caring about yourself might seem a selfish way of beginning to rediscover love. However, most psychotherapists and also the great wisdom traditions of the world would agree that this is where it needs to begin. If you don't love yourself you'll feel miserable and unintentionally spread resentment, anger and generally bad vibes around you. Here, therefore, are some of the steps you can take to make sure you really, really love and value yourself.

Be OK

To make the journey out of depression, it is going to be important that you have a basically friendly, loving and accepting attitude towards yourself.

You need to have this even if you have made all kinds of mistakes in the past or have let yourself down in some way that you now feel thoroughly ashamed of. You can be sure of one thing. If at the time you had had the capability to do better, you would have done. Everyone is doing the best they can at the time.

You can also make sure that you have a positive attitude to yourself even though you are good at some things but not so good (or even completely hopeless) at others. That's natural. No one is good at everything.

Unfortunately, inherently hostile and even vicious attitudes to self are common. Sometimes they are deeply buried - coming out in snide ways such as cynicism, sarcasm or vicious judgements of others. Check to make sure that none of these feelings about yourself could possibly apply to you:

Hostile attitudes to self

- Inherently bad
- Undeserving

- Not good enough
- Unlovable
- Dirty or unclean
- Useless
- Talentless
- A failure
- Unattractive
- Not worthy of inclusion
- Insignificant
- Too clever/stupid, upper class/lower class, rich/poor, educated/uneducated, white /black etc.

As you can see, the mind's capacity for self-abuse is considerable. When that happens the situation is made worse when you unintentionally prompt other people to join in the same negative and abusive attitude towards you. That's why some people have a tendency to get beaten up, passed over for promotion, bullied, despised or simply disliked over and over again.

OKness test

A way to check that you know that you are fundamentally OK is to see what happens next time someone asks to take a picture of you. Does your unconscious say: 'Help! It will show how awful I am' or does it does it say 'Well, if you want to witness my beauty that's OK'?

How to be OK

A useful way to appreciate yourself is to look at yourself (as well as everyone else in the world) from the point of view of what is right with you rather than what might be wrong.

Built into the fabric of the universe is an almost limitless number of qualities for each of which we humans have given a name - such as love, courage, persistence, caring, helping, creating, initiating, relating, wisdom, integrity, tolerance, being great at maths and so on. Each one of us has a unique mix of these qualities. No one of us can possibly have all of them. Your supposed faults and shortcomings are simply the consequences of the qualities which you do not happen to have been born with or to have yet developed. You really cannot reasonably beat yourself up about not having all of them. Gaps are inevitable. You and the rest of the universe really could not be any other way.

ACTION

List your special qualities.

Celebrate them and be grateful for them.

Now take an irrevocable decision that you are fundamentally OK. If you wish you can force this decision into your deep unconscious with an affirmation which you repeat to yourself any time you need to. Examples are:

- I'm OK
- I am lovable/worthwhile/deserving/ beautiful/acceptable/talented/proud to be who I am etc.

You can invent whatever affirmation exactly contradicts any negativity that you have about yourself.

You may feel that acknowledging your own personal beauty is a step too far. However, if you look beyond whatever may be appearing on the surface to the essence of any living creature you come across, you will see their incredible beauty. The same applies to you. So allow yourself to acknowledge your own personal beauty.

Hints

If you struggle to feel OK about yourself, it may help you to consider how and why a negative view could have developed. Here are some possibilities:

- Somewhere in early life you were mistreated. This could have been by parents, brothers or sisters, school mates or teachers. Since you were too young to fully understand what was happening you incorrectly assumed there must be something wrong with you rather than them.

- No one really appreciated and mirrored back to you your special qualities. Unsurprisingly, you never learned to appreciate them yourself.

- Your mother was depressed when you were born.

- A negative view of self was an inherited family attitude.

- Failures. Your mind has assumed that failures indicate that something is wrong with you, when in fact they are completely inevitable if you take part in life.

- Perfectionism. Some people have a tendency to strive for perfection all their lives. Since perfection is impossible they fail and then get down on themselves. The solution, for them, is to develop the quality of compassion for failings and imperfection.

- Sexual or physical abuse.

- Mad religious ideas that humans are inherently bad.

If you feel that any of these, or something similar, could have happened to you it may be helpful to identify exactly what happened as precisely as you can. Then work hard with affirmations to retrain your unconscious to stop beating you up and instead celebrate your basic value, beauty and qualities.

Love your feelings

If you are very unhappy due to depression you may be thinking that you must be splendidly in touch with your feelings. Well, you are in the sense that you are painfully in touch with the sum total of all of them ('very unhappy') but you aren't in the sense of being aware of the exact individual feelings. If you were accurately aware of the individual feelings you wouldn't be depressed - you would just be aware of the individual feelings and taking action in response to them.

If you are aware of individual specific feelings, you do not need to be depressed.

There are hundreds of feelings. Every one of them is a piece of software that has arisen through evolution in order to serve a useful purpose. This useful purpose is to tell us whether a particular situation is good or bad for us, and very often to guide us to carry out the exact action that will improve the situation. For example, if you sit on a hot radiator a message will rapidly arrive to get off it. Feelings are useful - but only if we are clever about them and don't allow them to coalesce into a ghastly featureless gloop that totally overwhelms us in misery.

If you aren't an expert at feelings please don't feel bad about it. Hardly anyone is! We go to school to learn maths or English or other subjects considered vital, but may not learn anything about such an essential life skill as coping with feelings. You can now begin a rewarding journey to become an expert at feelings. Before we look at how to do this, here is a summary of the advantages of what you are about to do:

Why it helps to become an expert on feelings

- Even in very bad situations, you don't have to get overwhelmed by horrible feelings. You can just notice each one of them individually and act accordingly. For example, you just lost your job and one of the feelings is fear; the fear prompts you to urgently look for another.

- Observing feelings is actually fun. They wander in and out of our consciousness all the time. They are wonderful and amazing as well as being extremely useful. You can do it in a few seconds any time.

- Paying attention to nice feelings is especially enjoyable. For example beauty, joy, love, appreciation, fun, admiration.

- Unpleasant feelings are friends too because they tell us that we need to take some action to fix a bad situation.

- Keeping potentially dangerous feelings like rage, hate, violence, murderousness or wanting revenge buried is like trying to keep a lid on a volcano. It's exhausting. Eventually the volcano may explode - which can be dangerous. So it's better to just lovingly acknowledge them. You don't have to act on them.

- Inherently riotous feelings like anger, mischief, rebelliousness, wanting to dance or sing or be thoroughly rude are often repressed due to a desire to be 'good'. This results in life denying joylessness. It's better to acknowledge them - but then act with care!

- There is a widespread impression - almost certainly correct even if unprovable - that repressed feelings can make us physically ill and also lead to mental illnesses such as psychosis, schizophrenia and bipolar.

How to notice your feelings

Turn your attention away from what's going on around you and towards whatever you can notice in your mind and body. You can do this for a few moments any time and any place - at home, in the car, in meetings, at a party, in the pub, in bed etc. A few seconds is usually plenty.

Try to find as accurate a name for each feeling that you notice as you possibly can. General names like 'miserable' or 'unhappy' aren't much good. Try to pin down each one exactly, for example 'jealous' or 'hopeless'. A list of some the feelings you might encounter follows.

Never judge a feeling as 'good' or 'bad'. They were all put there by evolution for your benefit. Trying to be a decent and loving person does not involve denying or repressing what you consider to be wicked feelings. It involves noticing them and then choosing to behave in a loving and skilful way.

Cultivate a sense of humour. Feelings are only software! You don't have to take them that seriously. You are not your feelings. You are the person who is able to observe your feelings and then take sensible decisions about them.

Try not to get bogged down in feelings. Ideally, feelings are like letters or emails. You look at them, take any necessary action and then move on. You don't spend the next few weeks or years (or even a lifetime) endlessly rereading them. I once saw a client who was depressed because he was still grieving the death of a niece 10 years previously. This was a feeling that should have been left behind long ago.

In part 10 we will look at some of the very advanced things you can do in order to have a chance of surviving the tumult of often extremely painful feelings that can arise in response to disasters.

Some common feelings

- Anger

- Grief
- Love
- Guilt
- Shame
- Hate
- Rage
- Fear
- Anxiety
- Contempt
- Desire for revenge
- Judgment
- Loathing
- Impatience
- Boredom
- Envy
- Jealousy
- Despair
- Disdain
- Arrogance
- Pride
- Hope
- Forgiveness
- Revulsion
- Resentment
- Rejection
- Like

- Dislike
- Joy
- Freedom
- Liberation
- Ecstasy
- Excitement
- Exhaustion
- Energy
- Anticipation
- Touched
- Sympathy
- Furious
- Cruel
- Desire to hurt/destroy
- Pain
- Suffering
- Feeling warm
- Feeling cold
- Feeling hard
- Feeling soft

There are many others! You can see what a fabulous range of software we possess, each piece with its own message and function.

ACTION

Lovingly notice your feelings.

Take appropriate action.

Stop a feeling once you have got the message and acted on it.

Love your anger

Anger is a force that arises from somewhere deep in our being whenever love (for oneself or others) is threatened and some kind of positive action is required.

Because anger is so closely related to love it tends to collapse along with love when we fall into depression. If this has happened to you, you need to reclaim your anger to help you to build, or rebuild, a life full of love. In a moment we will look at how you can do this, but first let's look at some of the occasions when it is helpful to welcome anger as one of our dearest friends:

Times to welcome anger

- Being treated unlovingly. For example, being on the receiving end of rudeness, bullying, injustice, insult, discrimination, lack of recognition when it is due, unfairness, corruption. It is natural to feel outraged and want to correct whatever has happened.

- You made a mistake. Your anger will tell you it was a mistake and drive you to correct it or at least try to learn from it.

- Someone stepped on your toe.

- You aren't living the kind of life you want to lead.

- You are doing something you don't want to do.

- You weren't brave enough to do or say what you felt was right.

- You didn't trust yourself enough to do what you wanted to do.

- You are witnessing (and possibly taking part in) humanity carrying out a global mass extinction of other species.

- You just spent 45 minutes trying to speak to someone on the phone about your electricity bill.

- Your partner didn't put the toothpaste away, didn't wash up etc.

- You want to go for a walk and your partner doesn't.

As you can see, anger happens about very minor issues, huge ones and all things between.

Enjoy your anger

Here is what you can do.

Practice noticing your anger. Anger is like a searing flame that rises from somewhere deep in one's body. It feels both powerful and tremendously purifying. Along with it comes a surge of adrenaline which, when we are healthy, leads to courage and action.

Try first to notice your anger about very small things. You could make a game, for example, of seeing how many times you can get angry before breakfast. Maybe (as previously noted) your partner didn't put the toothpaste away, the toothpaste is running out so you will have to buy more, you're late, the bath needs cleaning, there is no time to make coffee, the bus is late, it's raining and so on.

Now notice and celebrate your anger about bigger things - for example, the kind of life you are leading, aspects of your relationship, climate change or unnecessary wars.

If you have difficulty noticing your anger, try asking yourself the question 'Do I feel good about this?' If you pay attention to yourself you will know the answer immediately. If you don't feel good about something, you are angry.

Reflect on whether something in your background might hold you back from feeling angry when you should be. For example, was there an unwritten rule in your family that you were only lovable so long as you weren't angry? Did you grow up in a family which always pretended not to be angry? Did you usually get what you wanted by being sweet? If any of these happened they may be holding you back from demanding what you legitimately want. As soon as you begin to reclaim your anger you will feel more alive.

Never pretend your anger isn't there because you are frightened of it. Anger is indeed very powerful. The trick is to use this power skilfully.

What to do with your anger

Common responses to anger are to either pretend it isn't there or complain. The first is bad for you and the second is almost invariably useless. Here is what to do:

Try to identify the cause of your anger. This can sometimes be difficult because our unconscious minds can routinely identify a problem long before we are consciously aware of it. So for a time we can feel furious without having the slightest idea why. You just have to work at it.

As soon as you consciously identify the cause of your anger, you will feel a huge sense of relief and an equally huge flow of energy. Now you can work out what to do.

Now be sure to take creative action to fix the problem if you possibly can.

If you can't take effective action because the issue is too big for you (for example the state of the planet) do anything at all that you can no matter how small. You will then feel better.

Primitive uses of anger

Because anger is ancient software, it can often prompt us to take kinds of action that are not permitted in modern societies - such as applying a rock to someone's head. Here's what to do:

Always pause before acting on anger.

Discriminate. In the society I currently live in, what is the most creative and useful action I can take?

Check: is this action going to help the situation or just do a lot of harm to me?

Be realistic. Anger always wants action. But unfortunately there are some situations where action is impossible or useless. A common example is 'whistle-blowing' in corrupt organisations which almost invariably results in destruction of the whistle-blower instead of the problem. You may sometimes have to overrule your unconscious and say 'Sorry. No action' and try to move on with your life.

ACTION

Notice and celebrate any time you are angry. Be fiery instead of depressed.

Always act on your anger if you possibly can.

Act on anger skilfully.

Forgive

If anyone (or lots of people) have done bad things to you in the past it is essential to forgive - no matter how hard you find it or how much you don't want to.

Forgiveness is not important just because some religions say it is. It matters because, if you do not forgive hurts from the past, you can be left with old feelings which can ruin your enjoyment of the present. Among them are:

- Rage
- Resentment
- Bitterness
- Sourness
- Lingering sense of injustice
- Desire for revenge
- Hate
- An unfulfillable longing for justice.

Our minds are often extremely reluctant to forgive. One way to get over this is to realise that each soul on the planet is at its own particular stage of development. A human soul at any one time may be like that of a scorpion, cuddly cat, cunning snake, hungry shark, lethal crocodile or dominant lion. A person can only really act according to his or her condition at that time. The way someone treated you was simply a manifestation of his or her condition at the time.

Sometimes, our difficulty is not so much in forgiving others as forgiving ourselves. All those screw-ups, lost opportunities, betrayals of our own core values, failures of courage, acts of daft stupidity etc. The same technique as for others works. At the time you were drawing on the resources and abilities you had at that time. OK perhaps today you might do much better. But that is now, not back then. So you had better forgive. The alternative is persistent guilt and shame.

It may be that your difficulty is not so much in forgiving yourself or a particular individual but the world as a whole - because of the dire state of some of it. You can use the same technique. Just realise that the world right now is at a particular state of evolution. It is acting in a way that it can't really help - at least until such time as it evolves to a higher level (which might take millennia or never happen at all).

A forgiveness practice

As this book proceeds I am going to introduce you to some techniques that are very advanced. You may not want to do them but I would like you to know that they exist so that you do at least have the option. They (or something like them) have all been done by people looking to improve their lives, in different parts of the world, for thousands of years. Here is a forgiveness practice you could try:

Find somewhere private, either on your own or with a few others if they are up for it. Kneel down with something soft under your knees. Now bend forward so your forehead touches the floor while saying the word 'Kyrie' meaning Christ (you can think of the word 'Christ' as referring to the actual person or as a symbol for the greatest and noblest possible part of your own self). As you bend forward, allow your mind to drift over anyone or anything for which you still hold resentment, rage or any other negative feeling.

Now rise to the upright saying the word 'Eleison' meaning 'mercy'. Feel the Christ (literal or symbolic of your highest self) saying to you 'It's OK. It doesn't matter anymore. Let it go'.

You can do this practice for as long as you can manage; 20 minutes or an hour if you can. You could do it first for forgiving others and then for forgiving yourself. It can be life changing - as if a great weight is lifted from you. You can reinforce the memory of this practice any time you want by going on YouTube and listening to your favourite version of the song 'Kyrie Eleison'.

> **ACTION**
>
> Forgive everyone.
>
> Forgive yourself.
>
> Forgive the world.

Aim forwards

When depressed, you may have a tendency to mull over events that happened in the past. Alongside each of these events is a full collection of often painful emotions that went with them.

Of course there can be value in coming to terms with what went on in the past. It can help to gain some greater understanding of them by talking to someone. But as soon as you are ready to move out of depression you need to make a complete shift. This involves leaving the past behind and moving all your focus and energy to creatively building the kind of life you want from here on.

Taking positive action in the present, and making plans for the future, is the best way to leave behind painful old memories and emotions from the past. Your circuits quite literally fill up with new stuff.

Some people refuse to let go of the past because they think that their store of painful memories and past experiences is who they are. They may find their identity in all the events that have happened to them. But memories are just memories. They are no more significant than all the old information stored somewhere on your computer or phone. You are the person who observes your memories. From now on, you can be whoever you like and do whatever you like.

Do what you have to do

If you have a bad episode of depression you may be given time off work by your doctor or employer. For a time you may find it almost impossible to do the things you have to do such as shop, cook, clean, wash up, pay bills and see people.

However, if you possibly can, try to keep the inescapable necessities of life under control. If you can't, can you at least contact a friend to do the necessary things for you? Could you even pay someone? This is really important because when the mundane aspects of life slip out of control that's enough to make anyone depressed just on its own. Your chances of recovery would be reduced.

If you can manage to do anything at all in the day, see if you can keep the necessities going.

As you continue with this book (especially in Part 10) you will discover that it is possible to function even when not feeling like functioning and even when feeling terrible. Feelings are just software remember? And moods are usually just software too. You can override them to keep the essentials on the road.

ACTION
However bad you feel, try to keep the practical necessities of your life in order.

Check your psychological environment

Attempts to help people suffering from depression usually focus on giving them pills and/or attempting to reshape their mental processes through various forms of therapy. However, the cause of depression may not be something wrong with you but something wrong with your environment. Therefore, it is the environment that needs to be fixed, not you.

L O V E

To really care about yourself, check first that none of these are happening to you at home:

- Do you feel despised/controlled, bullied/discriminated against?

- Do you get physically or mentally abused in any way?

- Are you doing more than your share of the work?

- Are you living the life someone else wants you to lead rather than the life you want?

- Are you living with someone who is depressed (this is depressing)?

- Are your qualities not seen and appreciated?

- Is there no warmth or love in your home?

If the answer to any of these is 'yes', you will almost certainly be depressed.

Solutions

Fix the problem. This is always going to be the best solution. One option is to try to clearly identify the problem and then discuss it with a view to action. If this doesn't work you could try having a row and then delivering an ultimatum. For example 'If you don't do your share of the work/support me in my goals/ take action to fix your depression etc that's the end of the relationship'.

You may find that a therapist can help you resolve issues. But you will need a therapist who is brave enough to allocate blame and advise change where necessary. Just listening compassionately won't shift anything.

Leave. If negotiation or argument don't work, you basically have two choices: Stay in the environment (and stay depressed) or leave.

Your wider community is important as well as your home. You might think that if the community you are living in is to some extent depressed you can somehow rise above it and be OK. This is unlikely. The reason is that all conditions of consciousness, including depression, are vibrations. We humans (along with dogs, cats and other creatures) naturally vibrate with one another. If you have trouble understanding this, you could think about being in a crowd in a riot, at a football match or in a gathering of people sitting around an authentic spiritual teacher awash in love. The vibrations are totally different - and virtually impossible to resist if you are caught up in them. So if you live or work in a community that is depressed, you are unlikely to be able to resist it. Check, for example, whether any of these apply to you:

- Do you live in a 'depressed area'?

- Do you live in a community where a lot of people live on benefits (where depression may be endemic)?

- Are the schools and other institutions in your area depressed?

- Are you part of a social group which is routinely exploited?

- Is the area you live in unsafe?

- Are you part of a community which is marginalised on the grounds of race, sex, colour, religion or anything else?

- Does your family have a history of depression? If so, are you still caught up in it?

A 'yes' to any of the above will probably cause you to be depressed.

Solutions

Because so many other people are involved, it isn't likely that you will be able to bring about any change. You may have to consider getting out of there. Try to go anywhere where there is positive energy. Go even if it means moving your home or your job, taking a drop in salary, experiencing a domestic upheaval and taking risks.

You may think that you owe loyalty to people around you. You don't (except of course to children). A bigger loyalty is to be part of a creative rather than a destructive environment. You can leave an unhealthy environment to die all by itself.

A bad psychological environment at work can cause depression too. Check:

- Do you work in a failing organisation or one that's threatened with closure or mass redundancies? If so the entire organisation is probably depressed.

- Do you work in an organisation which is in a state of continual chronic overload - for example, some care homes and hospitals?

- Do you work in a profession that basically gave up years ago because the task is impossible - for example, some social work and teaching in some schools?

- Do you work in an organisation that has no interest in the welfare of its employees?

- Does your organisation have an unhealthy culture e.g. bullying, sexual discrimination?

- Does your work involve selling something basically harmful such as cigarettes, junk food, pointless drugs, unnecessary chemical-based farming methods, destruction of the environment, corrupt financial services, mistreatment of animals?

- Do you work for an arm of government that seldom or never achieves anything at all?

- Is there an absence of vitality and enthusiasm?

If any of the above applies to you, look for a new job.

ACTION

If you are in a psychologically depressed environment, change it if possible.

If not, find the courage to leave it if humanly possible. Find a dynamic, creative and healthy one.

Check your physical environment

Your physical environment can cause depression just like the psychological environment. Even the bricks and concrete around you can give off depression. Some council estates, for example, seem to have been put there by depressed people with the semi-conscious intention of making anyone who inhabits them equally miserable.

Do you live or work:

- In a damp basement with not much light?

- Next to a noisy road?

- Under a flight path?

- In a rundown council estate?

- In an area with no green space?

- In a flat/house/office full of chemical and/or electromagnetic pollution?

- In a hideous tower block?

- Under pylons?

- Under a mobile phone transmitter?

- With no windows or fresh air?

- Surrounded by ugly buildings and environment?

ACTION

If you are miserable in a place like one of the above, this would be a sign of health not ill health. Move if you possibly can.

Search for joy

Some of what has just been described is rather negative - about things you need to avoid if you possibly can. But now comes one of the most important and positive things you need to work on. This is to discover any flickers of joy in your life that you possibly can. You need to actively search them out and then as fast as you can let this joy spread into every other corner of your life.

Joy matters because it arises when your love is alive and managing to express itself in action. The more you can find it, the further you are along the road to a wonderful life.

There is something peculiar about joy. Human beings are in general fairly similar; we mostly have much the same feelings, fears and goals such as to survive, have friends, achieve, have a relationship, have children and so on. We are all constructed physically along more or less the same lines. However, when it comes to what gives us joy we vary a lot. What brings joy to one may mean nothing to another - and the other way round.

Do you know what gives you joy?

Could it, for example, be one of these?

- Dance - if so which?
- Visiting beautiful buildings
- Music - and if so what sort?
- Art
- Sport - and if so which?
- Exercise classes
- Walking
- Nature
- Mountains
- Sea
- Sailing
- Cards
- Games
- Parties
- Clothes
- Jewellery
- Gardening
- Making things
- Fixing things
- Science
- Maths
- Politics
- Healing
- Literature
- History
- Archaeology

- Animals
- Birds
- The stars
- Chatting to neighbours

There seems to be no end to the variety of what can give a person joy. If you know what brings you joy, do it now. Seek it out even if you are in the deepest misery of depression. It will reactivate your love and remind you that life can be wonderful.

Do you not know what gives you joy?

There are basically two things you can do:

- Check your past. Was there ever a time when you experienced joy? If so, what happened to it? Could you rediscover this kind of activity or situation?

- Use intuition. To find out what gives you joy, you need to use intuition. *Thinking* about what might bring you joy is unlikely to get you anywhere. Try as many activities as you possibly can until your intuition tells you: 'Yes! I love it!' Don't let your mind get in the way if the results are not what you expect.

Have you never experienced joy?

This can happen for a number of reasons. Perhaps you grew up in a joyless family or other environment. Perhaps you had an utterly miserable childhood. Perhaps it was just bad luck that you happened never to experience an activity that brought you joy. Here is what you can do:

- Try things as described above.

- Try to notice the smallest flicker of joy that arises from anything. You will feel a small stirring in your heart and mood. Keep paying attention to this feeling. Do anything you can to encourage it.

- If you are fortunate enough to be seeing a therapist, he or she should notice any time when you light up and become radiant when talking about some activity or other and reflect this back to you. This can help you to recognise joy and identify what triggers it for you. Don't despair; your joy will be there somewhere even if it was deeply buried.

- Ask a friend or family member if they have ever seen you light up with joy or enthusiasm. If so what caused it? Sometimes others notice more than we do ourselves.

Hints

- When you find an activity that gives you joy, you may encounter fear – perhaps because you're embarrassed to do something so unexpected. Joy is too important to let initial fear get in the way.

- We humans often have an innate terror of allowing others to see who we really are (in case we get wounded at a level we don't feel we could survive). Common areas where this happens are dancing and singing. It may take courage to allow yourself to fully engage in whatever brings you joy.

- It could be that you enjoy something that your friends don't. For example, you might enjoy Tai Chi while your friends find it boring or silly. Do it anyway.

Suggestion: Take joy seriously! It's more important than success or anything else. If you are joyful the people around you will be too.

ACTION

If you know what gives you joy, do it. No matter how miserable you may be feeling right now, force yourself to go out and find it.

If necessary, discover what gives you joy - then do it.

PART 4

Love Others

Key points

See people

How to see people when your mind tells you not to

Skills for introverts

Confidence

Focus outwards

See qualities not faults

Don't say you're depressed

If you are depressed, you might think that caring about other people is not exactly your priority right now. You might even be thoroughly fed up with other people or prone to feeling totally overwhelmed by them. Perhaps you have withdrawn from seeing even friends and family.

As soon as you can, it will be helpful if you can begin to consciously rekindle your love for others. There are at least two big reasons for this.

One is that caring about others will lead you naturally to wanting to spend time with them. Time with others is essential for your recovery.

Another reason for caring sufficiently about others to want to spend time with them has to do with finding a sense of meaning in your life. *Thinking* when alone about what, if anything, might make life worthwhile is unlikely to yield results. Meaning and enthusiasm arise spontaneously in the course of relating with other people.

The next steps describe practical things you can do to love others and delight in their company.

See people

The first thing you need to do is plan human contact. You need to do this even if for the moment you don't feel like it.

You can't love people in the abstract while lying alone on the sofa or out walking alone in the mountains. You can't do it on the internet either - you can't see into a person's eyes, get a sense of a person's essence and beauty, communicate beyond mere swapping of information, feel their warmth or enjoy a hug. So you have to get out there in the real world and see people.

Let's begin with a quick check to discover how much you manage to be with people at the moment.

Check

I spend time with people at home (husband/wife/ partner/parents/siblings/children etc):

o Every day
o Most days
o Sometimes
o Never

I spend time with people outside my home who are not family:

o Every day
o Most days
o Sometimes
o Never

I spend time with people I meet to have fun with or share an interest with (e.g. hobbies, sport, dance etc):

o Every day
o Most days
o Sometimes
o Never

I spend time with people I meet to do with the work I do:

o Every day
o Most days
o Sometimes
o Never

To be happy, you really need to be doing all of the above at least most days. If there are difficulties due to Covid please see 'How to Survive Lockdown' on page 189.

Of course it can be wonderful to spend time every day with children and/or a parent or close family member. But this isn't enough. We also need regular contact with people from the wider community, such as from work, sport or other activities. We need to see friends, acquaintances, strangers and colleagues. How is it for you at the moment?

You may object that some people, such as people undertaking spiritual retreats, can apparently be all right without seeing anyone. Well, what they are doing is exploring human consciousness - which can be scary to say the least. If their exploration goes well, they will eventually have a greatly enhanced capacity for intimacy with others. Just being alone simply leads to deepening depression.

If you are suffering from a level of depression that has caused you to withdraw and have less social contact than you need, the way back can seem daunting. Friends may have given up on you (or you think they have). You might have lost your job. Lack of money or health may be additional factors in causing you to be isolated. Circumstances such as working from home or being a single mother or being old can make the goal of being with people seem even more unattainable. A health emergency like COVID-19 may impose temporary limitations. However, there is always a way. Here are examples of activities you can get involved in which will bring you into contact with others. All of them and more will almost certainly be available in your area:

Job

Any job that involves meaningful relationships with others.

Hobby groups

Gardening

Model aircraft

Needlework

Historical society

Book clubs

Dance - numerous kinds

Crafts - numerous kinds

Ball games

Bowls

Tennis

Badminton

Squash

Football

Rugby

Hockey

Exercise groups/classes

Nia

Tai Chi

Pilates

Yoga

Gym

Cycling

Running

Swimming

Canoeing

Aerobics

Boxing and martial arts

Climbing

Arts groups

Singing

Music

Painting/drawing

Sculpture

Photography

Theatre and acting

Drumming

Spiritual groups

Church

Other religions and spiritual traditions

Yoga

Meditation

Sweat lodges

Chanting

Voluntary work and community service

Charity shops

Meals on wheels

Caring

Hospital reception

Youth work

Etc indefinitely

Games

Bridge, dominoes etc

Hints

- Join a group, society or activity of your choice which meets preferably once a week.
- Make a commitment to turn up. Make this in addition to your exercise choice.
- If you join something that happens less than weekly, join something else as well.
- You can use the internet, local adverts etc to help you choose what to join.
- When you've chosen, make contact and sign up immediately.
- Join something that feels like it might be fun. If you can't find something that feels fun and interesting at the moment, join anything.
- Turn up for local events – even if they don't particularly interest you.
- Try to use your phone and other media every day to keep in touch with people and arrange to meet. Never assume that they will not want to meet with you.
- The pub is not enough. You need meaningful interaction with others that goes beyond just talking or drinking.

- If you have just a lost a partner who organised most of the social contact, take on the job yourself.

ACTION

This is my plan for seeing enough people:

I'm going to join ....

The cost will be ....

I'm going to go with .... or alone

I'm going to begin on ....

How to see people when your mind tells you not to

There is no one on the planet for whom the giving and receiving of love is not their ultimate longing and source of happiness.

Unfortunately, when depressed, our minds have a tendency to present us with thoughts that do not accurately reflect what we really want. This is because, due to bad experiences, they have concluded that there isn't any hope. They may then set about justifying this by coming up with all kinds of stories such as:

- I don't really want any loving relationships anyway.
- I don't like seeing people.
- No one wants to see me.
- I am incapable of going out.
- Nothing will give me any joy.
- I never get accepted.
- The people I know are boring.
- Chatting to people on social media is a substitute for going out.
- On my own, I will find out who I really am and deal with my problems.
- The world is so awful that I don't see any point in joining it.
- People always let you down.
- We're all about to get nuked anyway.
- On my own I'll get closer to God.

If you can stand a bit of jargon, the above are what are known as 'rationalisations'. At first glance they can look reasonable. However, each of them is actually a trick devised by the mind to avoid owning up to what it is really saying which is something like:

I have had such a rotten time that now I absolutely refuse to take any positive steps to be happy.

The solution is to observe any false stories your mind is coming up with and make a choice to dismiss them. As soon as you start relating again your mind will recover. It will then tell you that loving and being loved was all it ever really wanted.

Hints

- You can be with people even when unpleasant feelings are happening. You are not disabled or incapacitated no matter how many unpleasant feelings are happening.

- Demote your feelings. Feelings are only software. They are not You. You are the person who observes your feelings. When you feel confident about that you can go out and be with others even though all kinds of difficult feelings are happening.

- Realise that you are acceptable. No one will reject you because you are experiencing unpleasant feelings. Everyone on the planet experiences at some time or another shame, exhaustion, anger, guilt, inadequacy, feeling a failure, feeling bad, feeling unlovable, shyness, feeling pathetic, fear, sadness, general misery and all the rest. Therefore, it is OK for you to be out there with everyone else.

- You don't have to say anything clever or amusing to be acceptable. Just be there. Trust that in time relationships will develop.

ACTION

Even if you feel absolutely terrible, try to see people anyway.

Skills for introverts

If you are an introvert, having a happy time with others requires more creativity than if you are an extrovert. Extroverts can be happy in just about any gathering. Introverts get drained in large gatherings. They tend to be happier one on one and in small intimate groups. They tend to dislike parties, dancing on tables, making speeches, singing songs round camp fires and being part of a jolly crowd. Here are some suggestions that may help if you are by nature an introvert.

- Plan situations that work for you and when possible avoid ones that don't.

- It's OK to be an introvert. In time, people will recognise your qualities.

- Introverts are important. It is probably true that they do most of the creative thinking. Extroverts need you to help them know what to do!

- Keeping in touch with friends may not come easily to you. A solution is to set up regular activities when you meet more or less automatically - clubs, sports, groups, dance or whatever.

- Don't underestimate the naturally outgoing types. They will see who you are and want you to be around. They don't want everyone to be extroverts just like themselves.

- No organisation could function without introverts. So be there.

- If you have to attend the sort of large gathering that you naturally hate, relax. Just put up with your discomfort without making it worse by beating yourself up about it.

ACTION

It's OK to be an introvert.

Plan what works for you.

Confidence

When depressed, you may feel dreadfully lacking in confidence any time you go out to see people.

Your lack of confidence may include feelings that you are in some way not sufficiently good looking, clever, talented, amusing, well, cheerful, successful, interesting, rich or remotely likely to be accepted or included. When that kind of mental stuff is going on almost any human contact can feel like hell.

A solution that is often proposed is that one should cultivate 'self-confidence'. This often comes across as attempting to convince yourself that you are in fact beautiful, successful, amusing etc as well as almost certain to win at anything, succeed at any job interview and get any promotion. This sort of confidence is, of course, daft. It's going to be shattered by your first encounter with real life.

Fortunately, there is another kind of confidence that you can cultivate. This is a deep rooted, unshakable and non-negotiable conviction that you are fundamentally and unconditionally acceptable. Here is what to do:

- Accept that you are depressed because life has dealt you some blows that you didn't yet have the skills to emotionally survive. The events that happened and your lack of skills were not your fault.

- Be proud that you are now learning skills that will in time enable you to be exceptionally resilient.

- Accept that, because of your depression, your mind is feeding you a load of negative information about yourself that is unjustified. Instruct it to stop.

- Decide that, like every other human being on the planet, you have an inherent value. This is unconditional. It is the case even when you are having a difficult time.

- Realise that you do not have to do or be anything to be unconditionally acceptable. You are OK just exactly as you are.

- Take a ruthless decision to the effect that if anyone decides that you are not acceptable it is their problem not yours. Don't buy into their sickness.

ACTION

Be unconditionally OK.

Focus outwards

When you venture out to be with people, try to take a break from looking inwards at your own personal and emotional problems. Turn your attention at least partially outwards towards others. If you don't manage this, you will bore others half to death, they won't want to be with you and in no time you will be back on your own and getting more depressed.

Try to avoid three common mental states which can make paying loving attention to others more or less impossible:

Anxiety

Anxiety is unacknowledged fear. It usually results in complete preoccupation with self to the exclusion of anyone else. When you can replace anxiety with a healthy normal experience of natural fear you can continue to pay loving attention to others. Here is how to do this:

- Happily admit to yourself that anxiety is fear. It is not some kind of special illness that requires years of therapy or medication to get rid of. It's just good old fear. There is nothing remotely wrong with being afraid (if you did not experience fear you wouldn't stay alive for long).

- Try to identify exactly the cause of your anxiety. For example, it might be about a job interview, the state of your finances, driving on manic roads, one of the kids being ill, your partner wanting to leave, your health etc. As soon as you precisely identify the cause of your anxiety it will turn into honest fear.

The generalised anxiety state you have been experiencing will disappear at the instant that you identify and own the fear.

- Fear demands action. Take action to fix the cause of your fear. This action does not have to be perfect or even successful. The moment you take any positive action this will release your energy and end your anxiety.

- Be willing to fight. Long running anxiety can be due to a refusal to engage in necessary conflict due to fear. Almost any kind of action is better than none.

- Confront existential fear. We all experience a certain continuous level of fear due to the fact that we know that sooner or later things will go wrong, our health will fail and in the end we will die. One has to honestly face this and then take a decision to enjoy life in the meantime.

- Calm down. One way to lower your levels of anxiety is medication prescribed by your doctor. Alternatives include yoga and/or meditation in a group, tai chi, music, dance, church, sport and vigorous exercise.

- Breathe. As described in Part 2, breathe fully and deeply. This will dramatically reduce your fear and enable you to keep functioning.

Panic attacks

Like anxiety, panic attacks get in the way of relating.

Panic attacks are caused by failing to breathe when frightened. So keep practicing your breathing. If necessary, get help from someone like a yoga teacher or Alexander Technique teacher. When you can breathe fully and easily, you won't have panic attacks.

Hysterics, tantrums and uncontained emotions

Over recent decades, it has become fairly widely accepted that it is helpful to be in touch with one's feelings. This is correct. However, it is not helpful to let them spill out all over the place. There are several reasons for this:

- You are dumping your emotions on others. If someone you met was having a nice day, he or she won't be anymore.

- They are *your* feelings. As the owner, you are responsible for dealing with them and taking appropriate action.

- Hysterics and other emotional outbursts are usually designed, more or less consciously, to manipulate others into giving you what you want. This is not love. It's manipulation. Sooner or later people get fed up with it.

The solution, therefore, is to honestly experience feelings while still making room to pay attention to others.

ACTION

Become expert at fear.

Contain emotions while still being aware of them.

Breathe.

See qualities not faults

The human mind is naturally expert at spotting anything that is not quite perfect. It will see in a moment the one imperfection in an otherwise perfectly painted room or display of vegetables in a shop. If permitted, it will do the same for people.

When the mind slides into this kind of negativity, love disappears. In its place come judgement, condemnation, fear, cynicism, hate and a complete absence of joy. Before long we can find ourselves habitually dividing the people we meet into 'nice' (because we haven't yet discovered their faults) or 'not nice' (because we have). Instead of a life of joyful intimate loving relationships, we are then caught in a life of perpetual distrust and conflict.

Here is what to do:

See qualities - when you meet anyone, look for their qualities. You will soon see that a person is, for example, kind, brave, persistent, flexible, tolerant, full of integrity or whatever. Try to deeply appreciate the wonderful qualities that they have.

See no faults you may say 'That is utterly ridiculous! I know people who are dishonest, selfish, manipulative and even downright evil'. You don't have to look at the situation that way. You can realise that what seem to be faults are actually simply qualities that are not yet developed in a person. For example, if a person tells a lot of lies it is just that he or she has not yet developed the quality of honesty; if a person is selfish it is because the quality of generosity has not developed; if a person is violent it is because he or she has not yet learned any gentler ways to deal with problems. Every 'fault' can be compassionately reframed as a quality that is not yet developed. In that way, you can appreciate everyone.

Accept that souls are not all in the same condition

It may be that you and your friends are far along a path of becoming loving, creative and harmonious human beings. But not everyone is. Some people, for one reason or another, are at a point where their main concerns don't go far beyond money, power and sex. You cannot really blame them for that any more than you can blame a crocodile for still being a crocodile. It is possible to love them - while keeping your wits about you in any dealings with them.

ACTION

See qualities.

Don't bore people with your depression

Depression has been widely promoted over recent years as an illness that can happen to anyone, a bit like flu or cancer. However the wider public, including employers, are not necessarily taken in by this. They know that depression usually occurs because someone has had a very bad time and hasn't been able to cope with it.

Therefore, be cautious about saying to one and all that you have unfortunately caught a disease called depression. They may not be particularly impressed. Since you are reading this book a negative view of you is also unfair, because you are in the process of getting rid of depression and being great to be with.

What you can do, when anyone asks how you are with apparent genuine interest, is say honestly what your feelings are. So you can say openly that you are furious, sad, worried, afraid or whatever happens to be the case. This will very likely evoke sympathy and even practical help. As you will recall, experiencing feelings is not depression.

PART 5

Be Loved

Key points

Believe you are lovable

Show that you are lovable

Be beautiful

Accept love

Trust

Don't think you know what others think

Patience

Check your neuroses

Check the parts that no one can like

Be in a family

Be in a relationship if you want one

Being loved is as necessary as oxygen, food and water. It brings energy, joy, warmth, comfort, confidence, security and a sense of meaning in our lives.

You might think that whether you do or don't receive love is up to the people you come across. If hardly anyone loves you, surely that must be because they are not very nice people? Actually, that isn't how it works.

Everyone longs to love just as much as they long to be loved. However, in order for a normal (as opposed to exceptional) person to give you love, you need to be open to receive it and to clear away any obstacles you might unintentionally be putting in its way.

You will find the suggestions in this part especially important if you have never had much experience of being loved. If that is the case, you may find being genuinely cared about confusing or even threatening. Do you find it hard to believe that your boss, employees, the police, doctors, politicians, teachers, staff in shops, neighbours or others genuinely care about you? If so there is every chance that they won't. You need to allow them to love and then they probably will.

The next steps are all about simple things that you can do to make sure that you are loved.

Believe you are lovable

If you have been suffering from depression you may have lost confidence in the fact that people out there in the busy world will love you. You may even no longer believe that friends or family or anyone else at all can possibly care about you or be bothered with you.

If you are now aiming to joyfully re-engage in the world, you absolutely need to believe that you are lovable. If you do, you will be loved. Anyone who knows they are lovable can go anywhere in the world and be almost certain to receive love and goodwill. Anyone who doesn't, will struggle to be accepted and may even have their worst fears about humanity confirmed.

Believing you are lovable means believing in yourself just as you are. This includes your faults, shortcomings, inadequacies, past depression and past mistakes. If it didn't, no one on the planet would be lovable!

So that's it. Believe you are lovable. If necessary, fiercely retrain your mind, by constant instruction and repetition, to believe unconditionally that you are lovable.

ACTION

Know that you are lovable.

Show that you are lovable

When depressed, it is easy to unintentionally slip into habits which give out signals to the effect that you do not seriously believe that anyone out there is longing to welcome and appreciate you.

Even if you don't feel like it at the moment, it will be helpful to, if necessary, put on a performance to show that you expect to be loved and included. There is nothing wrong with giving people some clues as to how you would like them to respond to you. Here are some things to check:

Appearance

It's embarrassing to write about, but look clean and don't be smelly. Wear cheerful clothes - especially not dull greys and blacks. If you look depressed people will be less likely to want to be with you.

Posture

Paying attention to posture went out of fashion with the Victorians. However, hangdog expressions and physical collapse give out signals of despair.

If you currently feel bad about yourself, put on a tall and confident performance anyway. Others will then respond positively to you, you will feel better about yourself and a virtuous circle begins.

Don't be habitually alternative

A few people really are different or highly original - and may well be accepted as such. Most alternative signals however are a message to the community that you think it is rubbish, consider yourself vastly superior and want no part in it. The community will duly oblige by rejecting you. Among alternative signals are piercings, tattoos, purple hair, being semi-naked, being totally covered up, hoodies in warm weather and rings in your nose or tongue. If you want to be cared about beyond a possible tiny circle of equally alternative friends, give out signals that you are actually willing to be cared about and included.

Manners

Old fashioned good manners make it easy for people to care about you. They needn't involve any sacrifice of your own personal integrity and independence.

Be involved

Even though depression may be telling you that you don't want to be involved, you need to show that you do. Once you are involved people will understand that you are not rejecting them.

Be positive

When problems arise, we humans divide into two groups. The first group complains. It complains about the boss, partner, businesses, products, services, landlords, tenants, politicians, the environment, the system, institutions and in fact just about every effort sincerely made by the rest of humanity. The other group sets about devising solutions. If you can be one of the second group, you will be loved and respected and have a great life.

Contribute

People throughout the world are on the whole proud to look after those who for one reason or another can't look after themselves. Although most are too polite to say so, they despise those who make no positive contribution when they could. So contribute in any way that you can.

LOVE

ACTION
Show that you are lovable.

Be beautiful

Seriously? It's possible that you don't look like a film star or a supermodel. On top of that depression may have led you to think everything about yourself is awful. So you wonder how on earth you could be beautiful.

It may help you to realise that what makes a person beautiful is not primarily their physical appearance. It is their light. A person who is happy and positively moving forward in their life is radiant; he or she actually emits light. This light is highly attractive to others - to the point where a very radiant person may have to take some precautions to avoid unintended physical relationships! Here are some things you can do to be light:

- Never allow yourself to feel shame about your body.

- Fashions come and go. If your body is not a currently fashionable one (for example you don't resemble a malnourished stick insect) who cares?

- If you don't feel bad about a disability, others probably won't either.

- Eat food that is full of light, such as fresh fruit and vegetables and to a lesser extent anything fresh and uncontaminated. You will then be attractively radiant.

- Don't take drugs. Drugs result in an aura that looks like dark sludge. People notice.

- Do the things described in this book to be happy. Depression is dull. Happiness is light and irresistible to others - no matter what you look like.

If you wish, you can do some very advanced practices to increase your light, such as this one:

Find somewhere quiet.

Become aware of your physical body. Feel it from the inside.

Now become aware of your more subtle (basically the electromagnetic) body. You will notice there is consciousness and awareness in it.

On the in breath visualise that light is entering your body from every direction in the universe, steadily increasing the light in you.

As your breath pauses before it reverses, visualise that this light is transformed in your being.

On the out breath, visualise that you emit your light to all corners of the universe.

Continue as you become more and more radiant.

ACTION

Love your body.

Increase your light.

Accept love

Love arrives in three main ways; through the heart, the eyes and actions.

Your heart

Because the heart is extremely sensitive we naturally, due to the frequent shocks and challenges of life, build up layers of defence around it. These defences are in the form of energy that is blocked instead of flowing and muscular tension all around the chest area.

To overcome this, try to allow your heart to be really soft whenever you are with someone. Literally welcome them into your heart. You will find further ways to soften your heart in Part 6.

Your eyes

Soft eyes receive love. Hard eyes repel it. So keep your eyes soft.

Allow people to see your eyes. If you hide them away by avoiding eye contact, behind sun glasses or in any other way, you are telling people that you do not dare to receive love.

Notice if you experience shame when others make eye contact with you. If so, continue to forcefully retrain your mind so it knows you are OK and quite naturally deserving of love.

Your actions

L O V E

As you more and more become involved in the world, loving actions will flow towards you all the time. However, if you have been depressed (and so for a time rather cut off from love) you may not realise this is happening. You may even misinterpret actions which are motivated by genuine concern for you as hostile or abusive. Here are examples.

Someone at home or at work takes the trouble to show you how to do something. You experience it as hostile criticism. It is actually an attempt to help.

You are devastated by being overlooked for promotion. It may be because you are most useful in the role you currently have.

You see a present as an attempt to ensure your compliance.

Being told off. May be because you really need to stop doing something.

Pointing out a fault. May be coming from love.

Rules. May be for your own good.

A boss points out some things you could improve. You see it as an insult; it is actually help.

Having something you wrote rewritten. May be a gift - so you can see how it could be done better.

Being told you did something badly. Maybe you needed to know that.

Help. Can be seen as an attempt to interfere.

Laws. May not be to control you but to protect you (for example regarding drugs or driving).

Correcting factual or logical errors.

Pointing out that your technique for playing your favourite sport is terrible.

A yoga teacher physically shows you how to do it right.

Being sacked. Even this can be a gift. Perhaps your job suited neither you nor your employer.

If you are in a negative state of consciousness all of the above can be interpreted as abusive. If you are open to love, you can experience them as gifts. If you can get in the habit of this, more gifts will flow towards you.

Trust

In order to be loved, it is necessary to cultivate basic trust in other people. If you don't, they will be offended. They may even be motivated to confirm your distrust by letting you down or exploiting you. Here are some things to check:

A bad past is not a guide to the future

You may have had experiences in the past of people who have proved to be untrustworthy. This might have been parents, teachers, brother or sister, pupils at school, business colleagues or others. If this is the case, your mind may have concluded that all people are inherently harmful, dangerous, ill disposed, exploitative, abusive or in some other way untrustworthy. This is false.

Base your experience on the people you actually meet (not on the people you once met, the people you have heard about or the ones you think you might meet).

Most people are OK

Radio, TV, newspapers and other media make money by scouring the planet for bad things that are happening and then telling you about them. This is not an accurate picture of the world. The reality is that about 99.9 % of the people on the planet are well disposed and kind.

The more you trust, the more you will evoke trustworthiness in others.

Trust is not the same as being naïve. Of course there is a chance that at some point you will run into someone, or some organisation, that wants to actively harm you. There is no need for this to erode your basic trust in people. All you need to do is watch out for the signals which are usually fairly obvious.

> **ACTION**
>
> Trust.
>
> You will then normally receive love.

Don't think you know what others think

Especially people who consider themselves sensitive (a lot of people who get depressed) have a tendency to think they know what others are thinking about them. As you begin to spend much more time with others, you may find yourself thinking things like:

He/she doesn't like me

Secretly despises me

Can see that I'm really depressed

Is just being polite

Can see how inadequate I am

Has better things to do

Doesn't like what I am wearing

Finds me unattractive

Wants to talk with someone else

Wouldn't like me to phone them up

Wouldn't want to go for a walk with me

Is angry with me

Is bored by me

If you invent thoughts like these in the minds of people you meet, you are likely to withdraw from them and put them off caring about you. The chances are that every one of those thoughts is a symptom of your depression rather than any kind of reality. Here are some sensible things to do:

- Distrust your mind. You don't know what others are thinking.

- Instruct your mind to always assume, as its default position, that others are well disposed to you. They probably are.

- If you really want to know what someone else is thinking, ask them.

Patience

If, due to depression, you are only now starting to go out more, you may find that some people immediately notice you and make every effort to include you. In no time you will have new friends and feel relaxed.

Another possibility, however, is that you are disappointed to discover that people you meet don't warm to you straight away. In fact, for a time they may not even notice that you are there at all. If this happens, it is not because anything is wrong with you and it is not because people don't like you or can't be bothered with you. There are several reasons why it happens:

- There is a natural human (and animal) caution about strangers. Just like dogs and cats, we sometimes need to be reasonably confident that a person isn't dangerous before trusting enough to engage with them.

- Any time you join a new group or circle of friends, you are asking to become part of an already existing system of relationships. It may be that that system works well and no one feels any particular need to change it. It is perfectly natural therefore if it takes some time to welcome you in.

- It isn't only you who is likely to be shy. Almost everyone you meet will be too when they first meet you. They may need time to get over this.

- When you meet new people, they may be busy talking with their existing acquaintances and simply fail to notice you for some time.

If people are slow to include you, it is important not to allow your mind to descend into paranoid thoughts to the effect that no one likes you, they are horrible people, you are basically unlikable etc. All you need is patience. Just be there.

One good way to be accepted is to give up trying to make any kind of impression on anyone. You will then inadvertently be yourself. People like that.

ACTION

Patience.

Check your neuroses

Neuroses are pointless, irrational and energy wasting things that we do. There probably isn't anyone on the planet who hasn't got a few of them. They can have the effect of turning people away from you, or at least annoying them.

Here are some common neuroses. You can check to see which you might have:

Fear of spiders/frogs/snakes/creepy crawlies

Always being late/early

Fear of flying (actually safer than driving)

Bottled water with you at all times

Food fads

Bizarre diets

Taking unnecessary pills

Constant washing

Obsessive exercise

Workaholism

Alcoholism

Drugs

You struggle to get rid of anything

Collecting pointless information

Fear of heights

Fear of crowds

Fear of confined spaces

Fear of dirt

Internet addiction

Checking your phone every few minutes or seconds

Excessive worry about the environment (actually fear of your own death)

Excessive health and safety

Aversion to risk

Trying to make everything perfect

Never going out without makeup

Attempting to maintain a perfect body

Obsessive religious and spiritual practices

What neuroses really are

The underlying purpose of a neurosis is almost always to avoid fear. It will probably be a very serious fear such as that of losing a relationship, being unsafe, losing health and ultimately death. None of us enjoys owning up to such enormous fears so it can seem a better option to persuade ourselves that everything will be OK so long as we eat no fat, wash hands every ten minutes, have another drink, go by train instead of air or adopt some other neurosis.

How to get rid of neuroses

Neuroses serve such a valuable function (avoiding fear and terror) that they are difficult to simply stop. If you do manage to stop a neurosis a new one will probably appear to do the same job.

The way to get rid of neuroses is to keep patiently, lovingly and compassionately noticing your feelings. You will need to take this gently but at the same time courageously. If you haven't discovered it already, you will eventually get painfully in touch with the fact that we are all terrified of such things as loss, ill health, being unsafe and dying. As soon as you can tolerate these ultimate fears, your neuroses will fade away.

The work of gradually acknowledging your most difficult fears can be done on your own. If you can afford it, psychotherapy can help. A psychotherapist is expected to undertake this work for him or herself and should therefore be qualified to accompany you on the same journey.

As has been said through the ages, facing up to the prospects of loss and eventual death are a key to the maximum enjoyment of life. It also has the effect of making a person ever more clear, uncomplicated and thoroughly enjoyable to be with.

> **ACTION**
>
> Keep allowing your feelings – especially fear.
>
> Be simple not neurotic.

Check the parts that no one can love

We are getting very advanced here. As we have said, people are basically loving and nice. But at the same time there exists in the human psyche an area of darkness. In it are to be found such things as cruelty, a desire to control and dominate, hatred/fear of the opposite sex (usually mixed up with love), aggression, violence, love of killing, love of war, sadism, primitive tribal and racial loyalties and the thrill of revenge.

Of course it is tempting to attribute this darkness to other people such as terrorists, religious fanatics, criminals or foreigners. Unfortunately this doesn't work. We all know it, are attracted by it and have it in us. The question is what to do about it.

Denial doesn't work

One strategy is to attempt to be good. That way, it's others who are bad. The problem is that the darkness is there whether we pretend it isn't or not. When we pretend it isn't, a huge amount of energy gets blocked. We become lifeless, joyless and judgemental of others. That doesn't make one very lovable.

Lovingly acknowledge it

The darkness is there whether we like it or not. As you continue to gently and lovingly observe your feelings and thoughts, you will come across it. Relax! Allow yourself, compassionately, to be fully conscious of it. Just accept that it is part of the human condition. As soon as you do you will find it loses any power over you. Eventually, it goes away to the exact extent that you want it to.

As you continue to engage in this somewhat alarming exploration of the human condition, you will become simpler, more straightforward, more radiant and easier to be with.

ACTION

Lovingly witness the full range of human feelings and thoughts.

Be in a family

To get the love you need, it helps to be in a supportive family. Your family can be a family of parents, siblings and cousins or a family you create.

If you don't have a family linked by genes, you can set about consciously creating a family. Gather together friends with whom you share interests and with whom you naturally resonate. Then look after them and keep in touch with them just as you would with a real family. This is much better than trying to forge your way through all the difficulties of life on your own.

To maintain your family, you could suggest meeting say every month at a set time. Then everyone just comes if they can without any need for an invitation.

Be in a relationship if you want one

If you have been depressed, you may have been tempted to think that a relationship could make you happy. That rarely works. A relationship will work when you have built a functioning life of your own and filled it with loving friendships. You are then in a position to choose who if anyone you might wish to share it with.

If you do have a relationship, or are thinking of beginning one, you might like to reflect on the things you will need to contribute to it for it to work. Here are some of them:

Love.

Harmony. There is an obligation to try to live together on the whole harmoniously. Without this life becomes hell.

Resolution of inevitable conflicts. Either peacefully or via the route of a row.

Warmth. Emotional warmth is deeply nourishing. The opposite is coldness which is chilling and life denying.

Respect. Respect for your partner's qualities, efforts, achievements etc.

Tolerance and understanding. For your partner's faults and shortcomings.

Support. Especially for your partner's goals and longings.

Celebration. Any time your partner achieves something that is important to him or her.

Hugs and cuddles.

Doing your share of the work.

Taking your share of the responsibility.

Helping each other to grow. This can sometimes involve loving challenge.

Independence. If you depend too much on your partner he or she will get fed up with it.

Making time for sex if it's important to you both.

Quote:

*'It is not for the love of a husband that a husband is dear,
But for the love of the Soul in a husband that a husband is
dear.
It is not for the love of a wife that a wife is dear,
But for the love of the Soul in a wife that a wife is dear.'*

Brihad Upanishad. Around 500 BC.

ACTION

Bring the essentials to any relationship.

PART 6

Open Your Heart

Key points

Open your heart

Relate through your heart

Notice your patterns in relationships

Live from your heart
Attune to happiness

So far we have been considering aspects of love that can all reasonably be brought into your life by means of a conscious decision taken in your head. As described in Part 1, you *think* about how your life could improve and then *decide* to love. That's a tremendously good start.

However, you can now enter another whole new dimension of love if you wish to. This is the love that comes from your heart. The 'heart' in this case does not mean the physical heart but the powerful centre of energy in the centre of your chest.

Western health systems are still rooted in 19th century science which saw the body as basically physical and chemical (accordingly, they treat illness using surgery and chemicals). However love, the central driver of humanity, is not physical or chemical. It is an energy located primarily in the heart. We all recognise this when we use everyday expressions such as 'heartfelt', 'coming from the heart', 'meeting through the heart', 'heart connection', 'warm hearted' and even 'heart broken'.

Everyone knows that Cupid fires arrows of love not into the big toe or the brain but into the heart.

If you can allow your heart to open, soften and become more and more powerfully alive you can expect some wonderful (and transformational) things to happen including:

- You experience love more deeply.

- A warm energy rises upwards into your brain causing you to feel happy.

- You discover that you can feel in your heart the condition and even sometimes the thoughts of others. In that way you can become much more sensitive to others.

- You can connect much more deeply with others.

- You become energised.

- Your experience of joy and beauty are enhanced.

- You discover that your heart is a centre of intelligence. For example, when you need to take a decision your thinking mind may come up with all kinds of pros and cons leading eventually to a decision. If you pay attention to the feeling in your heart you may discover a different (and more intelligent) decision.

- Your entire body and mind begin to resonate with love.

How to open your heart

Find somewhere where you can be on your own for a few minutes, so you can concentrate.

Withdraw your attention from whatever is happening around you.

Try to feel inside your body. See what you can feel, first, inside your head. You will notice that you do have some kind of awareness there. Now move your attention to inside your throat. See what you can feel there. Now move your attention to inside your chest. See what you can feel there.

Move your awareness from the physical sensation in your chest to the more subtle electromagnetic aspect of your

LOVE

heart region. You will notice there is consciousness and awareness there too.

With each in breath, imagine that your heart softens a little. With each out breath, allow it to totally relax and let go of anything it might be holding on to.

As you repeat this, you are likely to notice constrictions around your heart. Over the years, it may have protected itself by building up layers and layers of defences so it may even come to feel as if encased in concrete. With each repetition, allow the constrictions to dissolve a little more.

As you continue, you may find that old memories and emotions surface into consciousness. Even if they are painful, don't worry about this. Coming into consciousness releases them.

You can keep doing this exercise every day, or several times a day or even for the rest of your life. With practice you can do it anywhere - when driving, in meetings etc.

Here is further practice that you could do:

Centre your awareness in your heart as before.

Now imagine a Being sitting just in front of you. This Being has the characteristic of perfect love. The Being you imagine might be one from history that you associate with perfect love such as Jesus or Buddha, someone you once actually met or entirely imaginary. Try to form a clear image of this Being. If nothing comes just wait patiently until it does.

As you breathe in, visualise a stream of perfect love flowing from the heart of the Being into your heart.

As you breathe out, visualise a stream of perfect love flowing from your heart and being received by the Being. Continue.

Note that as your heart opens, it may release long held emotions, feelings and memories. These may be temporarily painful but then they go and you become simpler, clearer and less burdened by past experiences and baggage.

The methods for opening your heart just described come from ancient spiritual traditions from around the world. If you want to you can take them much further. You will discover an advanced, precise and sophisticated science that works with the very subtle energies to be found in the mind/body. You can find it in traditions such as yoga, tantra, Sufism, native American traditions, shamanism and no doubt many others less widely known.

Possibly the most powerful of all these techniques is the Sufi one of whirling. You can see it on YouTube. It works by swirling the energy in the heart and so releasing it. Practices like this are very powerful and need to be done in a safe environment led by a teacher who knows what she is doing. You can find them if you wish to.

Relate through the heart

There are basically two ways of relating with other people.

The most obvious of these involves exchanging information by means of words. This might involve talking, texts or emails. That's how we discuss football, catch up on local gossip, get the news and do business deals. It happens through one's head and isn't all that different from two computers exchanging information. It doesn't lead to relationships of much depth.

A deeper form of relating is through the heart. Our hearts are super sensitive instruments through which we feel others. We feel them and they feel us. Love flows between our hearts. This is what is known as 'heart connection'. This is when deep, intimate and warm relationships happen.

Next time you meet anyone, try centring yourself in your heart and feeling and inviting the connection between you. Then you can do this with everyone, for the rest of your life.

Try going for a walk down your street with your heart open. See what happens.

You can keep on deepening your ability to relate by continually working to further open and soften your heart.

Notice your ways of relating

As you enjoy relating more and more, you might find it interesting to notice some of your habitual ways of relating. You might notice that some of the habits you have picked up in the course of your life are not helpful or no longer seem appropriate - in which case you can choose to change them.

Here are some examples of habits that you might want to change or at least modify:

You get extremely close to someone and then feel an urgent need to pull away.

You decide a person is absolutely wonderful and then abandon them when you discover they have shortcomings just like everyone else.

When upset you go off on your own and never share your feelings/thoughts with anyone.

When upset you dump it all on whoever is nearest.

When upset you have hysterics which sooner or later causes the other to leave.

You long for love but when it happens get terrified of intimacy.

You dare not love for fear that it will one day end.

You tend to feel great by depending on someone else. Eventually either they or you get fed up with this and the relationship ends.

You never allow yourself to get close to anyone.

You never trust anyone.

You trust absolutely and eventually discover that no one can give you what you want all the time.

You keep being attracted to a kind of person with whom a relationship could only be disastrous - for example an alcoholic or someone you feel you could rescue.

You merge your life with someone else's but then your soul's longing to be itself makes you angry and drives you to leave.

You divide people into 'good' and 'bad' – with occasional reclassifications.

Because you were once bullied/abused/despised/ controlled/rejected or whatever, you tend to think people are doing it again. They probably aren't or if they are it is because you are unintentionally inviting them to.

You smother people with love.

When you love you aren't much good at showing it.

You love with your mind but not so much with your heart.

You keep your heart closed because of fear.

You feel controlled when you are actually being cared about.

How do you tend to relate with others?

To change a habit that isn't useful, all you need to do is to become consciously aware of it. From that moment you need never be a slave to it. Here is a simple example. You notice that you have a tendency to walk out of relationships, whether at home or at work, as soon as you start to feel bored. Next time you feel bored in a relationship you can decide to deal with it differently and less destructively (an intelligent course of action might be to take steps to stop feeling bored).

Live from the heart

You can now realise that the essential you is located right in the centre of your heart. From now on you can 'live from the heart'.

You can pay attention to your heart. It is the centre of your intelligence. It feels everything around it. It tells you how you are. It informs your brain about what is worthwhile and what isn't.

Your brain is now going to be a servant and useful instrument of your heart. Any time you feel yourself flying up into your head, relocate to the heart.

Any time you are anywhere, check to see if the essential awareness of 'I' that is you is located in your heart or somewhere else such as in your head or even somewhere way above your head in the stratosphere. If necessary, relocate yourself into your heart. It is a better place to live from.

You will discover that the more securely you locate yourself in your heart, the more you feel connected to others and the whole world around you.

Attune to happiness

Your heart produces a powerful energy that makes it easier to tune your awareness to happiness.

Happiness, like all other emotional states such as fear or distrust, is a vibrational frequency rather like a frequency of a radio station. You can deliberately choose to tune yourself to the frequency of happiness. It is a real thing - just like your favourite station on the radio.

Have you ever wondered why some people almost always seem to be happy and to spread happiness around them? They do this because, consciously or unconsciously, they habitually tune themselves to happiness. You can do that too.

You may object that no one can, or even should, be happy when something really bad happens such as loss of someone you love or one of life's other disasters. However, even when you are suffering, your underlying attunement to happiness can remain. Even if it goes for a time it can remain at least as a memory so you know you can return to it when circumstances allow.

ACTION

Open your heart.

Relate through the heart.

Notice your patterns in relationships.

Attune to happiness.

PART 7

Love Your Work

A job is a great antidote to depression. Even if you don't need money it brings social contact, challenge, teamwork, achievement, recognition, growth, friends, excitement and at the very least something to do all day.

Just about any job is better than no job. But one of the greatest sources of joy would be if you could find work that you really love. In case you don't yet have this, here are some questions, the answers to which will help you get clear about the work you would love:

Do you like working for yourself or for others?

Do you naturally like office work, hospitality, caring, business, healing, organising, manual work, intellectual work, writing, managing, serving, designing, working with animals, cooking or what?

Have you ever met anyone about whose job you felt jealous (jealousy tells us what we would like but haven't got)?

Is there any activity that you have always found easy? For example, drawing, accounts, cooking, children, computers, growing things? Things are easier when they suit us.

If you didn't have to go to work, what would you choose to do all day to have a wonderful time? Could it be the basis for a job?

Do you currently have a hobby which is more fun than your job? If so might it become a job?

What would you like to wear at work? Suit, jeans, overalls, uniform, smart, casual, indoor, outdoor?

What sort of environment would you like to work in? Indoors, outside, office, workshop, factory, call centre, nature, farm, animals, forest, computers or what?

Do you like travelling or not?

Do you like working alone or in teams?

Do you like working at home or away from home?

Big organisations or small?

Government or private?

Commercial or not?

Are you doing what someone else wanted for you when you were young (for example parent, teacher, social class, family tradition)? If so, what do *you* want?

If you didn't care about status, money or responsibilities, what would you do all day?

Is there a contribution to the world that you would really like to make? If so, what?

Are there tools that you would really enjoy working with? For example, computers, phones, chainsaws, carpenters' tools, builders' tools, tractors, diggers, cranes, pen, saucepans, cookers, calculators, spreadsheets, lathes, lab equipment?

What qualities do you especially enjoy manifesting in the world? For example, caring, fighting, negotiating, creating, planning, serving, organising, selling etc.

Are you naturally interested in money? Do you like working with it?

Have you ever thought 'I would love to do that if only it was possible'? If so what was it?

Was there something you wanted to do which you abandoned because it didn't fit in with your idea of your social class, education or what you thought you were capable of?

Is there some need that you can see in the world around you which you would love to help with?

Are there people you especially enjoy being with? If so, what sort of people are they and what do they do?

If you were a member of a Neolithic tribe, what would your ideal role have been?

As human consciousness evolves, certain jobs that used to seem worthwhile might now seem to you useless or even downright harmful. Can you think of new kinds of jobs that would seem really thrilling to you? If so, what are they?

The job I would love

Use your answers above to describe the sort of job you would love. For the moment, try not to get bogged down in considerations of what might be realistic. The first thing to do is to dream.

ACTION

Start looking around. Apply for jobs or start your own. Use any contacts you have.

Remember that any movement at all in your preferred direction will make you feel a whole lot better.

If necessary, use your spare time to retrain for what you would like.

L O V E

If you don't see much hope of getting what you want, go to Part 9.

'Let the beauty of what you love be what you do.' Rumi.

'Work is love made visible.' Kalil Gibran

St Augustine: 'Do what you love.'

PART 8

Love Your Lifestyle

L O V E

It would be nice, would it not, if you could love your entire lifestyle as well as your job?

Perhaps you've been smart enough or lucky enough to fashion the kind of life that you want. But is it possible that your life is not what you really want? You might try to rationalise your current situation by saying something like: 'This is just the way life has to be. I have to pay the rent, get on the train, spend my time as I do, live where I do...' and so on. But rationalising doesn't work if you're denying any genuine needs that are unique to you. Deep processes operate in the human psyche that won't be taken in and can make you miserable.

To be clear about what you really like, try answering these questions:

Do you like living in a town or in the countryside?

Do you like being by the sea, on the sea, in mountains, inland, in a valley, by a river, by a lake or what?

Do you like being in 'civilisation' or the wilds?

Have you ever read a book or seen a film which left you thinking: 'I'd love a life like that'? If so, describe it.

Have you ever met anyone about whose life you have felt jealous (jealousy tells us what we would like but haven't got)?

Do you care about fashion?

Do you think that current human lifestyle took a sensible direction? If not, what would you have preferred?

What sort of climate do you like? Hot, cold, mixed, wet, dry, humid, sunny?

Any preference about altitude? High, low or even underwater?

Do you like travelling or not?

How much company and social life do you need?

Do you naturally go to bed early or late?

Was there anything wonderful that you dreamed of as a child – but it never happened?

What sort of landscape do you love to be in? For example trees, sea, hills, mountains, valleys, rivers, forest, buildings, cities, towns, villages, remote, busy?

Would you like to be in your country or somewhere else? If somewhere else, what is it that you like about it?

Have you ever thought 'I would love that kind of life if only it was possible'? If so what was it?

What sort of people would you really like as your friends?

What sort of community would you really like to be part of?

If you were to win the lottery and go totally mad, where would you go and what would you do?

If the modern world did not exist, what might have been better for you?

This is the life I would like

Use your answers above to describe it. You could write, draw, describe to a friend or even make a model.

ACTION

Make any movement at all towards the life you would like.

If getting there seems unrealistic, turn to the next part.

PART 9

How You Might Get What You

Never Thought Was Possible

Getting what you want, in any aspect of life, can sometimes seem daunting or even impossible. Here are three ways that might enable the seemingly impossible to happen:

Imagine the solution

Imagine in as much detail as you can the job or lifestyle that would be your ideal. When caught up in the daily struggles of life, it is easy to never get around to this. But imagining what one wants is the essential first step in achieving anything at all.

Find a large piece of paper and draw a picture of your ideal. This could make it even more real.

If you prefer words, you could write a short piece describing your solution in detail. Or describe it in detail to any friend who is willing to listen. The more detail you can include, the more real and attainable your solution will become to you.

As you imagine your solution, try not to get distracted by thoughts of how on earth you could possibly get there. The first job is just to picture it.

Now take any action whatsoever, no matter how small, in the direction you would like. This will already make your goal seem just that bit more attainable.

Now keep taking actions, no matter how small, in the direction you want to go. Eventually, you will discover that you have arrived.

Make sure the obstacles are not in your own head

The obstacles to getting what we want usually seem to be out there in the outside world. As often as not they turn out to be in our own minds. Check for obstacles that might be in your mind such as:

- No one in my family has ever done anything like that
- People will think I've gone crazy
- I could never do anything like that
- What about the kids?
- I've got so many commitments here
- My partner wouldn't agree
- I'd take a huge drop in salary
- I'd have to begin all over again
- What about the cat?
- My friends seem perfectly happy doing what they do, so why shouldn't I?
- Everyone seems to think I'm doing really well - so why change anything?

Is something in your head keeping you trapped in a life you don't want?

If you still feel trapped in a life you don't want, try asking yourself: 'What could stop me making a new life herding yaks in Mongolia?'. Your mind may come up with a hundred reasons. However, if you persist, you will eventually discover that the answer is 'Nothing'.

You may feel that doing work and having a lifestyle that you love is selfish. Actually, being happy and expressing your unique talents in the world is the biggest contribution you can make to others.

Develop a quality you need

You might feel that you could never get what you want because you just 'don't have what it takes'. In other words, you lack some essential quality. In that case, here is how you can develop any quality you need:

Identify any quality that would enable you to get what you would love. Examples are:

- Courage
- Persistence
- Overcoming inertia
- Power
- Willingness to change

- Confidence to learn new skills
- Confidence to use contacts and network
- Confidence in the ability of humans to adapt to something completely different
- Application
- Hope

Qualities needed for a specific job such as caring, patience, routine, reliability, imagination, service, managing, ordering, controlling, innovating, studying, selling, negotiating.

Now find somewhere quiet where you can concentrate for a few minutes.

Focus on the quality you think would help. You will notice that every quality has a distinct vibration. See if you can feel intensely the vibration of the quality you want.

Now invite the vibration of that quality into your being. Let it resonate through your entire body and mind. You may notice some initial reluctance because for one reason or another you are not yet tuned to that vibration. Invite it in anyway, as a new honoured guest.

Resolve that from now on your chosen quality is going to be part of you and you are going to express it in your daily life.

Keep practicing using your new quality. Along the way you will need to learn new skills in its use and will doubtless make mistakes. Keep learning and practicing.

You will notice that 'You' do not necessarily need to be the person you thought you were. You can be whoever you want to be.

Enjoy conflict

In order to get what you want in your life, you will often have to engage in conflict. This might be with one person or a group of people who in some way or other are preventing you. There is nothing wrong about this. In fact it is inevitable because you and others may often have sincerely held opposite opinions.

If you hate conflict, tend to avoid it or just can't do it you will seldom get what you want and need and will therefore be depressed. So the question is how on earth you could possibly enjoy conflict and get good at it. The solution is to learn to engage in conflict not with rage or hate but with love and genuine concern for the other. You can actually completely disagree with someone or do the opposite of what they want you to do while keeping your heart open and genuinely caring about them.

To do this, here are some of the ways to do conflict. You can reflect on which you are already good at and which you might like to develop. The fuller your tool box, the better your chances of having the life you want:

- A disapproving look.
- Saying 'No'.
- Saying 'I don't agree with that'.
- Finding the courage to say very clearly what you want (or don't want).
- Daring to ignore main stream opinion if necessary.
- Talking the issue through. Deeply listening to the other – then doing what you feel is right.
- Very direct and fearless eye contact while stating your view.
- Never, ever tolerating being bullied.
- Choosing to express anger when necessary, either slightly or extremely.
- Attuning your energy to power if you have to.
- Creating a force field to dominate the other if you really have to. This is subtle but works.
- Being very rude if this is the only way to preserve your integrity (for example government or corporate corruption).
- Legal action.

- Violence as a last resort (for example a child being harmed).

Some of the very best fun you can have in your life is when you and someone disagree about something very important and, as a result of discussion and conflict, you together arrive at a brilliant solution which neither of you could have arrived at on your own. This is how almost all great creative projects are achieved.

PART 10

How to Emotionally Survive

Very Difficult Times

Depression is often brought on by something going badly wrong - loss of someone you love, loss of a job, failure of a business, bankruptcy, illness or becoming homeless. It's as if one or more of your essential needs for happiness has just been brutally stripped away.

When these things happen, here is what you can do to prevent inevitable unhappiness leading to depression. When you can do that, you can keep on coping with life so that the whole disaster falls behind you as quickly as possible.

Take action

When something bad happens, people are often encouraged to seek help with the emotional consequences, perhaps through counselling or medication. However, the first thing you probably need to do is take some very practical action.

For example, if you lost a partner you just lost half of a team; he or she might have been the one who earned the money, managed the house, took the kids to school, did most of the cooking or rewired the house. Now you or someone close to you is going to have to take on those roles.

In a similar way, if you experience the catastrophe of losing a child or someone very close to you, you may have to rapidly build a new social network and support system. An accident or illness might require a big adjustment to your life. Losing a job or business is going to lead to a financial crisis which will require action.

Whatever the disaster, you need to redesign your life as quickly as possible. To do this, you may need to learn new skills and do things you have never done before. Note that it is possible to take necessary action even when very emotionally distressed.

Take exercise

After a disaster you will experience a flood of horrible feelings together with all the hormones and physiological changes associated with them. You can reduce these by taking vigorous exercise. If you can force yourself to go out and have fun as you normally do, that will help too.

Survive your feelings

Now we come to an advanced skill that will enable you to survive even very powerful and unpleasant feelings without allowing them to develop into depression. This skill is to anchor yourself in your consciousness rather than all the things it tends to get completely caught up in.

Find somewhere quiet. Sit still. Get rid of any distractions like music, children or pets.

Now be aware of anything at all that your consciousness is noticing. It might, for example, be sounds, smells, aches and pains, thoughts, feelings, memories, plans or ideas.

Now ask yourself just exactly who is noticing all that stuff. It is, of course, you. Identify with this you, not all the stuff it is noticing. Enjoy experiencing it. This is who you really are.

You will notice that the 'I' that observes feelings (and anything else) is stable and unchanging. You will also notice that it feels fundamentally OK. This is true even when the world around you is not OK. So the more you can identify with the essential 'I' that is you, the more stable and fundamentally OK you can be.

Have some fun trying to explore to the very centre of your consciousness. See if you can locate its centre. Try to really be there. Just be aware of being conscious.

Every time your consciousness attaches itself to one of the things it habitually notices (thoughts, feelings etc) just pull it back and return your awareness to just your consciousness. Note that of course you cannot observe your consciousness - only consciousness can observe. But you can be aware of it. With practice you can do this for longer periods.

You will find this easier to learn if you attend a meditation class.

The more you can identify with your consciousness, the essential 'I', the more you can withstand the ceaseless play of feelings and emotions that arise in the course of life. You can still act on them when you need to.

Go to the heart of the problem

Here is a way to turn what seems to be a horrendous time into a gift. It takes courage and concentration. If you can possibly do it with a counsellor or therapist who you like and deeply trust that would be great.

Head for the nearest sofa. Make yourself warm and comfortable. Get rid of any distractions. Pay attention to your breathing for a bit to quieten down.

Now ask yourself this question: 'What is **really** the problem?' Wait until an answer comes. Say it out loud. If you are with a therapist, ask him or her to repeat your answer very briefly just to help hold your concentration. Do not allow comment.

Now ask yourself the same question again: 'What is **really** the problem?' If someone is with you ask them to repeat your answers each time.

Repeat for at least 30 minutes. Each time you are looking to access a deeper level of the problem. Eventually you will reach all the way down to what is really the problem in your life that is making you so miserable.

Just contacting the problem with clarity and consciousness will probably be enough to relieve the suffering. It might also lead to action to fix it.

PART 11

So You Just Got Depressed for No Apparent Reason

Key points

Feelings triggered by events from the past

Sensible precautions

Disasters that happened long ago

Even when a life is full of love and nothing of any apparent importance has gone wrong, it can happen that seemingly out of nowhere a person gets struck down by depression. What the hell happened? Here are two possible reasons – together with what you can do about them:

Feelings triggered by events in the past

What happened was that an event that you might not have even consciously noticed scored a direct hit on a raw spot in your unconscious. Almost certainly the event will have been:

- Something someone said
- Something someone did
- Something that just happened
- A particular smell or other physical sensation

When a raw spot gets hit the result is that painful feelings from an original bad thing that happened get triggered all over again. As a result, even if it is a beautiful day and everything is going well, you can find yourself inexplicably miserable.

If you sometimes fall into depression suddenly and for no apparent reason, here is how to stop it:

First of all remember that this happens every now and then to just about everyone. It's often played down with expressions like 'having a bad day' or 'feeling under the weather'. So you don't need to make the situation worse by feeling bad about it.

Now try to notice that you just fell into depression for no apparent reason. It isn't just 'One of those things'. A serious event is happening in your unconscious.

Carefully review everything that happened in the last few days. See what feelings and emotions arise in relation to each one. For example, you might feel anger, grief, resentment, a dip in energy or that your breathing constricts. You may notice that there is some kind of emotional intensity around an event even if you can't yet identify the feelings exactly. Don't take any notice of your conscious mind if it says: 'Oh, that was just a little thing and it didn't matter at all'. Just pay attention to your feelings. Try to spot the event, however trivial, that triggered something in your unconscious.

Allow yourself to really feel the feelings/emotions. As you have already discovered, when you can really feel them you don't have to be depressed any longer; you are now just experiencing natural feelings, which means you can keep functioning.

See if any memories come. Can you remember what caused the raw spot in the first place? For example, was it the teacher who said you were stupid? Was it your mother who you felt despised you? Was it the car crash that terrified you when you were little? Was it the bully at school? To help you identify the raw spot you can refer to the examples coming up in a moment.

Allow yourself to experience the authentic feelings around the triggering event - if you can identify it. When you can honestly experience the feelings they get processed and eventually go away.

If possible, share your discoveries with someone. This always seems to help.

You will find that every time you manage to identify a triggering event, a sort of miracle happens. The depression goes! While to begin with it might take you days or even weeks to work out what happened, the time comes down to hours or even minutes with practice.

Then, any time you feel your energy begin to collapse and the beginnings of depression set in, all you have to do is say to yourself: 'OK, here we go again! Who did it? What did they say? What happened? Who scored a direct hit on that boring old wound?'

When you can do that, and get the answer in minutes because you are now an expert, you won't get triggered into depression any more.

Sensible precautions

As a matter of common sense, try to avoid situations in the future where the kind of thing that triggers you into depression is likely to keep happening. For example, if being bossed around triggers you into depression, don't form a relationship with anyone who has a tendency to boss you around.

You can sometimes actively prevent events that tend to trigger you into depression. For example, you could say to your manager 'If you yell at me when I screw up I tend to freeze. If you make suggestions about how to do better I probably will'.

Here are examples of some typical wounds from the past that can leave a raw spot that might trigger you into depression when someone (probably completely accidentally) touches it:

- You weren't loved
- Someone abandoned you/stopped seeing you
- Cruelty, abuse, bullying
- You felt controlled

LOVE

- Loss of something/someone very dear to you
- You felt unwanted
- Frustration - not getting what you want when you want it
- You felt excluded/an outsider
- Trauma - such as an accident
- You felt despised
- You weren't listened to
- You were laughed at
- You were with someone depressed/ mentally ill
- You felt ignored
- Failure
- Rejection
- You were discriminated against
- You weren't respected
- You weren't appreciated
- You were left out
- Someone else got the credit
- You were taken for granted
- Anger/rows/conflict
- Absence of love
- Absence of warmth
- Rows
- Lying
- Being disliked
- Injustice, cruelty

- Being in an on/off relationship

What might trigger you into depression?

Disasters that happened long ago

Some disasters can be so bad that the feelings just won't go away. For example, you were abused in some way, beaten, not loved, despised, rejected or grew up in an environment devoid of emotional warmth or loving touch. The result is that the feelings stay around and prevent you from loving your life in the present. If that happens, you can try the following:

Make an enormous effort to live your life creatively and joyfully in the present. It's a bit like constantly pouring clean water into a container of dirty water. Eventually the nasty old feelings get displaced by new ones.

Try incredibly hard not to act out destructive old patterns of behaviour which arose in response to the original disaster. For example, try not to resort to violence, being bullied or abused or perpetrating either of these. Try to adopt loving patterns of behaviour even if they feel initially unnatural and unfamiliar.

You may be able to get over past hurts by consciously finding in the present what you were missing back then. In particular, the greatest healer for everything is love.

L O V E

Love in the present can make up for absence of love in the past. If you can find it and afford it, long-term psychotherapy might help. Over weeks and years you can be lovingly re-parented. You can discover what it is like to be in a warm, loving, stable and secure relationship. If you do take this route, you can expect it to happen in four stages:

1. First you may fully experience painful feelings and memories from the past.

2. You can gain some understanding of what happened, why it happened and what the effects on you were.

3. You now need to do something which may be very difficult, which is to forgive both others and yourself. You have to do this because otherwise you will remain trapped by the past and possible unhelpful feelings such as rage, grief and resentment.

4. Decide to love in the present - despite what happened in the past. And build a new and healthy life.

PART 12

Love Life

Since you have read this far, you are hopefully no longer depressed. Your life is filling up with loving relationships together with work and activities that you love and you can see a way forward for things to get even better.

You might think that from here on life is therefore going to be easy. Well, actually, because of the direction you have taken, you are going to meet some new challenges.

Here is the problem. If a person's ability to love is limited to self and perhaps one or two close family or friends, life in the current world is relatively simple. You just fight like hell for the wellbeing of yourself and those few close people you care about. But when your heart opens more and more to all people, all other living creatures, the environment, the climate and the planet living gets a whole lot more complicated.

There is no need to despair about this. Trying to do the best one can is just about the most fun and the biggest source of satisfaction that anyone can have.

What follows is an introduction to some of the issues you can expect to meet. In the case of everything you have read so far we have been resting on ancient knowledge; you can find guidance about what to do in psychology books such as the Bhagavad Gita and Greek, Buddhist and Chinese texts written more than 2000 years ago. But even the geniuses from the ancient world can't tell us all we need to know about how to live in today's world which is so profoundly different. So it is up to us to find solutions.

You can decide to love these challenges. If you believe in something one might call a soul, they are how the soul can learn and grow.

Manage your consciousness

If you have ever owned a boat, car or property you will know that they need constant looking after if they are to function well. Your consciousness is the same.

Almost all of humanity is currently addicted to doing a huge amount of thinking together with gathering, storing and processing information. That is why people like computers and phones - because they enable us to do even more of them. This cognitive condition of consciousness is exhausting and provides very limited satisfaction. You need to make time, therefore, for other more nourishing conditions of consciousness. Here are some of them:

Love. Read spiritual books, listen to relevant podcasts and be in any gathering where there is love. If there is love in your local church or other place of worship, go there even if you don't believe a word of the teachings. You might find love in all kinds of alternative health treatments whether or not you have any confidence in the science. Be anywhere where there is a vibration of love.

The sacred. Similar to love but a softer, more rarefied and otherworldly energy. Like love, we need it as much as water and air. You might find it in sacred music, sacred places, sacred ceremonies, sacred gatherings or nature.

Idealism is a very fine vibration where we search for perfection. You might find it in a discussion or spiritual group. You might find it in high mountains where there is just the extreme purity of bare rock and perfectly pure snow and sky.

Music, dance and movement. The human spirit longs to find expression and freedom through the body. Living all and every day in your head is not enough.

Using your hands and body as well as your mind

Stillness. Our minds are refreshed, and become more intelligent, by times of stillness. Moments of stillness may happen naturally but you can make them happen more often by attending a meditation group or even a meditation retreat. When your mind is still, you will notice that the resting state of consciousness is happiness (in the psychology of India, the word for this is

'Ananda' which means bliss). However busy your life, you can go back to this condition when you wish.

Light

As you progress from depression into joy, you will naturally become more radiant. This light needs to be looked after as you become more stretched by full involvement in everyday life. Here is a practice you can do on a daily basis to increase your light.

Find somewhere quiet where you can concentrate for a few minutes.

Turn your attention away from whatever is happening around you, and away from whatever your mind is busy with. Turn it inwards to your heart.

As you breathe in, imagine that your heart is filling with light.

As you breathe out, imagine that this light is radiating out from your heart into the far corners of the universe. If you are interested in contemporary science, you will know that it very possibly actually is.

With each breath, visualise that your light is becoming more and more beautiful and intense. Now you can extend your awareness of light to your entire body and mind, and even your near surroundings. You are becoming a being of light. Whenever you wish to bring a gift to other people, this is just about the best one you could bring.

When you do practices with light you are likely to inadvertently increase your quality of magnetism. This requires humility. If your ego attaches itself to your light and magnetism – that's narcissism.

Continue to soften your heart

As you get busier, you will get knocks and your heart may respond by wanting to close and protect itself. But this will be the opposite direction to the one in which you want to go. So you will need to help it to keep opening. You can do this with the help of the breathing practice described in Part 6. You can do it frequently - in the shower, in bed, while driving or whenever suits.

If you can, spend some time every year in a community that practices for example yoga, shamanism, Tantra, Sufism, Native American traditions or any religion that is a religion of the heart.

The balance of soft and hard love

The more you are involved in life, perhaps taking on all kinds of responsibilities, the more you will need to try to balance two very different aspects of love. Love can be soft, gentle, docile, giving, accommodating, compromising, harmonious, tolerant, patient, warm and cuddly. When you really care about others and the world around you love can also sometimes be fierce, powerful, authoritarian, terrifying, strong, determined, persistent, courageous and even ruthless. In order to create anything it is often necessary to destroy what was there before. So we struggle constantly to balance these two faces of love.

Seeing unexpected bits of yourself

The more you keep opening your heart and increasing your light, the more often you may become aware of bits of yourself that you don't like. This is something to celebrate. An ancient analogy helps to explain this. It is as if from time to time you look into a dark room that contains some not very attractive junk. If you don't have a light with you and just close the door again, that junk isn't going to bother you. In fact you won't even know about it. But if you bring a light with you all the junk is instantly revealed.

Fortunately, this is where the analogy stops. You don't have to do a lot of work to get rid of the junk. In the case of your psyche, just seeing it will cause it to fade away.

You will naturally find that you don't want to act on it any more.

Opinions collapse

If you have been lovingly noticing your feelings at an ever deeper level, you may eventually notice that what you thought were sincerely held opinions were actually just leftover feelings. Your political or religious opinions, for example, may turn out to originate from leftover rage, resentment, envy, entitlement, tribal loyalty, hatred of authority or a childish longing for certainty leading to signing up to some doctrine or other. You may feel empty and lost for a time. But then you discover a new, deeper and more authentic source of guidance.

Freedom can be frightening

You don't need to worry about this. What to do is not written for you in any book that you can consult and there is no teacher you can ask. But it does emerge as you go along. You just search deeply in yourself and search for what direction feels OK. Here is an old story that may help you to understand this:

A man (possibly only a man could be so stupid) walks miles through the jungle to see his spiritual teacher. After some inspiring hours it is time to return home. But it's dark. He cannot see his way through the vast and dangerous jungle so dashes back in and explains the problem. 'Don't worry', says the teacher, 'Here is a torch to light your way'. But on going back outside our hero notices that the torch only lights the first few steps of the way. He can't see the whole journey ahead. So he returns complaining that the torch is useless. His teacher explains that, for every step forward he takes, the light of the torch will move forward correspondingly. So he will easily find the path.

Be alone. A price of freedom can be that you sometimes feel very alone. No one is there any more to tell you what to do. You are no longer comfortably supported by someone else's values and opinions. However, there is a paradox. The more detached you are from all that goes on around you, the more you are free to love it and lovingly engage with it.

Expect transitions. The more you love the more you are likely to grow. This process of growth can sometimes lead to changes as profound as adolescence or moving into adulthood. In these times your values, goals, interests and enthusiasms may change. For a time you will feel confused and lost. Sooner or later, the old life falls apart and is no longer sustainable. Changes of this magnitude can happen to people in any situation in life. They are sometimes referred to as midlife crisis but can actually happen at any time.

If something like this happens to you, one way to think about it is as like the experience of a beautiful oak tree that loses its leaves in autumn. An ignorant tree doctor might try to help with all kinds of remedies to get the tree back to how it was in the summer. A more informed tree doctor would just wait patiently (providing any possible support) until all the invisible changes that happen in winter lead to an even more magnificent tree in the spring.

Expect suffering as well as joy

As your heart opens, you will experience not only your own suffering but that of the people around you and ultimately the whole of humanity and the planet. Of course there has always been suffering but there are special challenges now because just about all living things and the entire environment are in the process of being destroyed.

While being aware of this suffering it is at least possible to build an environment of joy around yourself. Being miserable because so many others are doesn't help anyone. And any action no matter how small that one can take to relieve suffering in some way helps.

It is also necessary to somehow accept that life on earth has never been, and presumably never will be, free of suffering. It has never been stable, permanent or safe. Civilisations collapse, epidemics strike, mass extinctions happen, death happens, the earth will eventually collide with the sun. The question is what to do in the meantime.

Win and lose

Life is like football. You win some and lose some. You can still enjoy the game. The only alternative is not to play at all. It's no good getting depressed each time you lose.

Conflict

Conflict happens when people with integrity disagree. It's inevitable. You can practice skills of lovingly engaging in conflict. The alternative is to live without integrity or commitment to anything.

Wonder who you are

When you see through your eyes, who is observing what you see? Is it some sort of software located in some kind of computer known as your brain? Or is some kind of universal consciousness looking through your eyes?

Scientists are struggling with this question. It matters because, if the second view is right, you are part of everything. You are everything. Everything is you. This could explain why you instinctively want to love instead of exploit or destroy. Keep up with contemporary science and don't necessarily take much notice of all the psychology, theology and metaphysics that went before. It might be out of date.

Who do you work for? Yourself or everyone?

Strengthen your ego

The ego is what enables you to function in the world and express your unique qualities in it. So you need to keep strengthening it. You might want to temporarily surrender your ego on a retreat in a deep state of meditation; but you will need it in stronger shape than ever as soon as you re-enter active life.

Manage desires

There is an aspect of our minds whose job it is to come up with desires. It tells us when we need essential things like food, water, love, exercise or something to do. However, it can easily lead us to want all kinds of things that we don't really need and won't make us any happier. Western consumerism relies on this. So it is worth observing this aspect of your mind very carefully to be sure of what you do and do not really want.

Doing deals

Doing deals is easy when you don't care about the other. But when the other matters as much to you as yourself, how on earth do you do a deal? You will be constantly trying to balance your needs with those of others.

Selling. Do you sell what you can or what will benefit the buyer?

Your life is your creative project

Perhaps the greatest creative project for all of us is to design an enjoyable and fulfilling life. But it's easy to get so caught up in activity that we forget. So it is helpful to review from time to time the life you really want.

A great way to do this is to write a poem (it doesn't have to rhyme or anything) entitled 'I have a dream'. What is your dream? What would be your perfect life?

The pain of loss

The more you love (a person, project, place, creature, nature etc) the more agonising the pain of loss. So how can you cope with that?

Start or join a community

A 'sangha' is a word used especially by Buddhists to describe a group of people who meet regularly to support each other. Even though people are changing, there are still dinosaurs out there who are bent on destroying our world, exploitation and the pursuit of harm. You have more chance of being happy and understanding your life if you belong to a supportive group.

Attune to the flow of human consciousness

Human consciousness continually evolves. Every one of us is influenced by the flow of collective human consciousness whether we like it or not. As a result, our opinions about what matters change and evolve.

Just now, we are living in one of those times when our collective consciousness is changing rapidly and profoundly. Many of the things which people thought were good to do even a few years ago, such as chemical farming, emptying the seas, shooting tigers, living off fossil fuels, exterminating wildlife and covering the planet in plastic, now seem totally mad. Many of the jobs we do are pointless or even actively harmful. We question whether our economic systems and institutions are fit for purpose. Status and reward appear to be inversely related to the usefulness of what people do. The lifestyles of many are possibly much less enjoyable than they would have been ten thousand years ago.

There are two ways to respond to this. One is despair and depression. The other is to regard the whole situation as a thrilling opportunity. You now have an opportunity to play a part in reinventing just about everything so that it does express the current direction of human consciousness. Especially if you are young, you have to try, in a way however big or small, to play some part in doing this. You will be challenged, but happy.

LOVE

Things I'm thinking I'd like to do:

L O V E

L O V E

LOVE

L O V E

L O V E

L O V E

L O V E

LOVE

L O V E

LOVE

ADDENDA

How to Survive Lockdown

If, due to Covid or for some other reason, you are unable to see people as much as you would normally, here are some things you can do.

First of all, do everything normal that you can. Meet whenever possible, exercise, eat, breathe, sleep and use the phone and internet to communicate.

If you are forced to be alone for a long time, you are going to find yourself doing something that normally through history only a tiny minority of people have done, which is to go on retreat. Here are some notes that may help you to not only survive but to enjoy a possibly life changing and life enhancing adventure.

What is a retreat?

Historically, 'retreat' does not mean a nice weekend away somewhere peaceful. It means turning your attention inwards to explore what it is like to be a human being. Since you are one, you don't need to study anyone else.

'Retreat' is actually a misleading word. For millennia periods on retreat (days, weeks or even years) have been used to find more in the way of happiness, peace and strength and subsequently contribute much more in the busy world. Perhaps a retreat should really be called an 'Advance'.

Who knows about retreats?

What follows is classical Indian and Middle Eastern psychology. That is to say, it is not psychology as practiced on a small island off the West coast of Europe. It's also from my experience of numerous intensive retreats.

First thing to do – build a secure foundation

To survive whatever you might experience on a retreat (feelings, traumas, questions, re-evaluations etc) build a rock in the centre of your psyche. Here is how to do it:

Sit down somewhere quiet, on your own, with your spine straight if possible. Close your eyes. Just sit still for a bit and relax. Now ask yourself a series of questions, slowly and with deep reflection. 'When I see, who notices what I see?' Search for an answer. Then 'Who notices what I smell?' 'Who notices what I taste?' 'Who notices what I feel?' 'Who notices my feelings and emotions?' 'Who notices my thoughts?' 'Who notices all the other stuff that turns up in my awareness?'

The answer, of course, is you. You are consciousness. Enjoy just experiencing consciousness. That's who you are. All that other stuff that you are normally probably so caught up with, is just stuff. Respect it but don't take it too seriously and try not to get caught up in it.

You can't observe consciousness (obviously, because consciousness is the observer). But you can experience it. Just be it. Feel at home. You will notice that it is stable. Never changes.

Naturally every few seconds, or minutes, or hours if you are expert, some kind of mental riot will start up (thoughts, plans, ideas, worries, memories etc). As soon as you notice a riot, dismiss it and return to consciousness. With practice, you can notice stuff just as it begins to arise and say 'No thanks, not just now'.

As soon as you can do this, even for a few minutes, you can survive even quite extreme circumstances with a degree of stability. Thoughts are just thoughts, memories are just stored information and feelings are just our inherited human software. They are not who you are. You don't need to take them too seriously. You become more resilient.

Any time you feel stressed or about to crack up, go back to this stable place.

You may find that chanting and spiritual music will help you into stillness. All on YouTube. You might find a meditation teacher you like on the internet. Be careful not to meditate too much; it needs to be balanced with activity.

Experience consciousness

You can have fun trying to find out where the consciousness that is you is. In the head? The heart? Everywhere? Is it yours or is it everyone's?

Notice what consciousness feels like. In India its characteristics are described as Sat, Chit and Ananda. That's knowledge, consciousness and bliss. Let's forget the first two for now because they are rather a challenge to Western science. 'Bliss' includes a combination of happiness and peace. Consciousness is inherently blissful. If you observe a cat on the sofa on a sunny day, you can confirm this scientific fact. Happiness is the default setting of consciousness.

Allow stuff into awareness

OK so now you are as strong as a lion. Cut off from other people and without shopping, parties, sport, work etc to distract you, stuff comes up. You wonder who you are, what you are supposed to be doing, what the point of it all is. Old memories surface. Maybe you relive ancient trauma. To your horror, you notice that you have been defining yourself by being a victim. You feel bored. You feel lonely and miss strokes and reassurance from others. You get depressed. You feel terrified. You experience despair. Then unexpected moments of bliss or even ecstasy. And so on.

Just notice it. Remember, as Buddha said, it changes. It will be different in the morning. Pay loving attention to whatever arises. When you do this, it gets processed and loses its hold over you. Never judge anything that arises as 'good' or 'bad'.

Now go back to your rock. One of the potential disasters of Western psychotherapy is that people contact painful stuff and then get stuck in it. Instruct your mind (a good servant but terrible master) not to. Like reading an e mail, when you've read it – bin it.

Allow more stuff into awareness

As you strengthen the rock of your consciousness by a few minutes (or hours) of reflection, it will tend to release more and more of the real experience of being a human being into awareness. Because you are now strong enough to survive it.

This process is often likened to the situation on the surface of a beautiful, calm blissful ocean. Every now and then bubbles rise from the depths and ripple the surface (to be honest, those bubbles are sometimes more like depth charges). But they pass and the ocean returns to calm and bliss.

In time, you will experience more and more of being human and, more specifically, you. This includes all the stuff that you don't like and may have comfortably thought only belonged to others. Never judge. Accept everything. Even very dark aspects of humanity such as violence, sadism, control, cruelty, envy, murderousness, tribalism, racism and so on lose their hold when you allow them fully into consciousness. All of these are only dangerous when unconscious and repressed – because then they can explode out in an uncontrolled fashion. That's when catastrophes like genocide and ecocide happen.

If you notice that some absolutely awful aspect of humanity is part of you (which it will be) you will be becoming a much more peaceful and loving person. This is why Rumi wrote the well-known lines 'The dark thought, the shame, the malice, meet them at the door laughing. They may be clearing you out for some new delight'.

But be careful who you talk to. You'll get scapegoated.

Benefits of opening to everything

These include:

Peace. You can spend more time in the bliss of pure consciousness. All that stuff doesn't bother you so much anymore.

You can be more loving and harmless.

If you do need one of the more disreputable aspects of humanity (eg violence, ruthlessness) it will still be there. Just under your control.

Vitality. Repression is exhausting. So is 'being good' and 'being nice'. Be riotously loving and creative instead.

Fears are better in awareness than repressed e.g. fear of death.

You no longer need to project parts of yourself you don't like or don't know about on to others. I remember, on silent group retreats, finding myself liking some people and disliking others. Since I knew nothing about any of them, I eventually realised I was not seeing them but bits of my own psychology. If you energetically hate anyone just now you're seeing bits of yourself you don't like. Lovingly hold that person in your heart instead.

Independence and courage. These come naturally when you realise that you don't need strokes from anyone else to be basically OK. This does not mean you become a loner. On the contrary, you can risk greater intimacy. And you can maintain your integrity in life.

You can have fun fixing any problems in your relationship. Relationships are like 19th century machines with cogs. If you change the cog that is you, the whole machine has to work differently.

You may find that your consciousness tunes (like a radio) to different wavelengths which you are not so used to. The predominant attunement on the planet at present is to cognition (thinking, information gathering and processing). That's why people are fascinated by the internet - so they can do more of it. Cognition is exhausting and mostly pointless. Never delivers meaning or joy. Enjoy it if you suddenly find yourself attuned to love, the sacred, idealism, God, nature or digging the garden.

Sitting in the fire

It has to be admitted that some unpleasant aspects of the human condition can take time to get rid of. Especially rage. So much rage is buried in the human psyche.

If it arises in you, congratulate yourself on allowing it into awareness. Fully experience it. I think it was Rumi who likened getting rid of rage to burning camphor. When it is set alight you just have to wait until it burns itself out. Daniel survived the fiery furnace. I remember interviewing the abbot of a Buddhist monastery for a TV programme. He was just like an abbot should be – serene, wise, loving, peaceful etc. He described how as a trainee monk he kept agitating to go on retreat alone in the jungle. There he would find peace, bliss and God. Eventually they let him. Every time he came out of meditation he found his fists were clenched, he was running with sweat and consumed with fury. That may have been his most productive retreat. My experience is similar. Now the rage is mostly gone – but still there if needed.

Forgiveness

You may find that powerful memories from the past arise. These can carry with them intense shame and guilt – about times you messed up or did something awful. You have to forgive yourself (forgiving others is relatively easy). You were just doing whatever you were capable of at the time.

Going deeper

There are practices that can enable you to turn even further within. They are not secret, but you don't want to do them unless you are in touch with someone who knows the territory. If you are interested, find a spiritual teacher who is trained within one of the established traditions. You need a teacher to guide and hold you – and if necessary to prevent potentially disastrous wrong turnings.

Experiences

People can have odd experiences in meditation (or for that matter any time). They can include experiences of your essential nature, of cosmic consciousness, seeing that everything is made of light or even feeling that you caught a glimpse of God. Possibly useful. But never strive for them.   Just relax in Ananda. Eventually, your entire being becomes suffused with light and love. There is a sort of indescribable inner warmth and inner knowing which transform yourself and your world.

Being useful

Since the 1960s, New Age spiritual teachers have been offering products such as 'enlightenment', 'illumination' or 'non duality'. Here's a question to reflect on. Is that what you want? Or is the Christian, Hindu, Buddhist, Islamic, Native American etc goal of loving usefulness in the world more relevant just now?

Imagine the future

Now an important bit. Just about everyone agrees that humanity is heading for disaster; the wildlife, the planet, the climate, then maybe itself. No point in complaining. The real fun now is to imagine how we would like things to be. That's what we need to do. That's how change begins.

Coming out of retreat

You may encounter considerable reluctance. Liking climbing a mountain, there can be great reluctance to return to the mundane world down there and engage in it. So – just do it.

It's OK to be alone

Here is the real ultimate reward if you can get that far. You may eventually discover that you don't need all the things you used to need – and even that you don't really need anything at all. What has happened is that you have internalised all the things out there that you thought you needed so badly. So you no longer need to dash around looking for love, success, reward, recognition, excitement, the perfect life and so on. Happiness is inside you. When necessary, you can be as happy alone as a 19th century lighthouse keeper away alone for months on end.

Michael Sclater

How Doctors Could Treat Depression

How would it be if health services were to treat depression in the sort of way described in this book?

On seeing a doctor a patient would routinely be prescribed sessions with a personal trainer together with gym membership (or equivalent) and expert help with elements of basic health including diet, breathing, sleep and money. The patient would receive a manual describing action to take and skills to learn. A counsellor, psychotherapist, life coach or other suitably qualified person would be available to help the person identify the problem in life that is causing the depression and take action accordingly. Help and support would be delivered personally and/or in a group. Patients would have access to specialist help in all areas covered in the manual. Doctors would be educated to understand that depression can be treated by enabling patients to take action, acquire skills and solve the problems in their lives that are making them depressed.

Acknowledgements

This book is a contemporary restatement of psychology that people have known for thousands of years. I would like to thank the remarkable people who have passed it on to me including especially Pir Vilayat Inayat Khan, Susie Morel, Dr Nigel Hamilton, Shantanand Saraswati, John Daly, Andra Goldman, Aziz Dikeulias, Swami Samarpanananda, Francoise Wright, John Fenteman, Munir Voss, Ted McNamara, Sue Arnold, Faye Peden, Chris Craig, the members of 'Innovations' and everyone I have ever seen for therapy. My thanks too to the Charlotte Hartey Foundation for financial support and encouragement.

About the Author

Michael Sclater trained as a psychotherapist at the Centre for Counselling and Psychotherapy Education in London, achieving registration with the UKCP in 1999. Since then he has seen clients for depression for the UK National Health Service and privately.

Since the early 1990s he has also intensively studied, both in theory and practice, the psychology of the East especially Vedanta and Sufism. He lives with his wife Pat on a beautiful hillside in North Wales where they are almost self- sufficient in food and energy. Recreations include climbing mountains and playing tennis for his county. His first career, after leaving Cambridge University, was in documentary films, winning a number of awards.

Printed in Great Britain
by Amazon

57817812R00122